Brink Road

Also by A·R·Ammons

Brink Road

P O E M S

A · R · Ammons

W · W · NORTON & COMPANY

NEW YORK   LONDON

For information about permission to reproduce selections from this book, write to
Permissions, W. W. Norton & Company, Inc., 500 Fifth Avenue, New York, NY 10110.

The text of this book is composed in 10.5 on 13.5 Adobe Garamond
with the display set in Futura Regular and Book
Composition by PennSet, Inc.
Manufacturing by the Maple–Vail Manufacturing Group.
Book design and title page illustration by Margaret McCutcheon Wagner

Library of Congress Cataloging-in-Publication Data
Ammons, A. R., 1926–
Brink road / by A. R. Ammons.
p.   cm.
ISBN 0-393-03958-7
I. Title.
PS3501.M6B75   1996
811'.54—dc20   95-42535
ISBN 0-393-31597-5 pbk.

W. W. Norton & Company, Inc., 500 Fifth Avenue, New York, N.Y. 10110
http://web.wwnorton.com

W. W. Norton & Company Ltd., 10 Coptic Street, London WC1A 1PU

1 2 3 4 5 6 7 8 9 0

for my wife and son

I am grateful to the editors of the following periodicals for first publishing the poems listed:

Abraxas: "Tenure's Pleasures"

American Poetry Review: "Focus"

Beloit Poetry Journal: "December Starlings"

Bluefish: "A Pretty Looking Sight"

Chelsea Review: "A Little Thing Like That," "The Many Ways Not Supreme"

Columbia Review: "Period"

Cornell Review: "Enameling," "Walking About in the Evening"

Epoch: "Serpent Country"

The Gettysburg Review: "Enfield Falls"

Grand Street: "Sparklings," "The Land of the Knobble-Jobble Tree," "The Deep Slow"

The Grapevine's Finger Lakes Magazine: "High Desiring."

The Hudson Review: "Loving People," "The Time Rate of Change," "Blues in the Valley," "Second-Rate Perfection," "For My Beloved Son," "Fall's End," "Summer Place"

Michigan Quarterly Review: "Obsession," "Lofty Calling," "Weightlessness"

Moosehead Review: "Changing Stations"

The New Republic: "Boon," "Putting On Airs"

The New Yorker: "Sentiment," "Ceppagna," "Day Ghosts"

North Carolina Literary Review: "Broad Brush," "Flat Rock"

The Ohio Review: "The Incomplete Life"

Panoply: "Getting About"

Paris Review: "Picking Up Equations," "Modes Against Too Much," "The Crystal Tree," "Death and Silhouettes"

Partisan Review: "Readings by Ways," "Museums"

Pembroke Magazine: "Regards Regardless," "Evasive Actions," "Superstars," "Rosy Transients"

Poetry: "Anxiety's Prosody," "An Improvisation for Soot and Suet," "All's All," "Hard and Fast," "Saying Saying Away," "The Clenched-Jaw School," "A Sense of Now,"

"Local Antiquities," "Collapsed Structures," "The Deep End," "Prey"

Raritan Review: "Downing Lines"

Science: "Microinscriptions"

Skylark: "Ontology Precedes Teleology"

Southwest Review: "A Part for the Whole"

The Southern Review: "Reading Ta'o Chien"

St. Andrews Review: "Pit Lines," "Abscission" (formerly, "The Separation")

Tar River Poetry: "Strings," "Prisons There and Not," "Moving Figures"

this end up postcards: "Establishment"

Times Literary Supplement: "Chosen Roads"

Verse: "Standing Light Up," "Construing Deconstruction," "Marginals"

Walking Magazine: "Walking Song"

Yale Review: "Middling Seasons," "Whitewater," "Spike-Tooth Harrows," "The Damned"

"Stand-In" and "Rarities" appeared in a limited edition as companion broadsides by Larch Tree Press. My thanks to James Tyler.

"First Cold" and "Looking Way Off" first appeared in the anthology *Poems for a Small Planet.*

Brink Road lies off NY 96 between Candor and Catatonk.

CONTENTS

Brink Road

A SENSE OF NOW

Rock frozen and fractured
spills, a shambles,

and tiers of time pile into,
shatter through

other tiers or angle up
oddly, brightly lined with

granite or talus, a jumble,
"metaphysical debris":

but the stream finding its
way down a new hill spills

along the right ledges, shifts
the schist chips about and

down with becoming coherence,
and moss beds down ruffling

shale edges dark gray
to green, and the otter

drinks from sidepools
almost perfectly clear.

PICKING UP EQUATIONS

Not smart to be out under trees with the wind still this
high: billowing & breaking bring down stob ends

of last year's drought-wood that died way up in the branches,
and a nick on the noggin could drop you, no one around

to see after you or call rescue, or you could just be
dazzled and wander off down the road, wild: still, don't

you like picking up storm cast, swatches of leaves snapped
off, bark rippings, to weight the wind's reach each thing

gave to, how high it held or hung, what angle brought
it down: one thing's certain, falls shadow the wind,
ellipses, sprung, noding downwind to the arc including everything.

ENAMELING

The ice-bound spruce boughs
point downward
as if to
slide their sheathes off:

the fairest morning
in weeks, crystalline,
yields to the fire
rising in the east:

even the smallest presences
take on orientation — lit
and shaded snow, twinkling
millions in starred

ground frost, dust-snow
highlighting twigs
lighting birds
flurry free to light on.

UP-COUNTRY

Their faces fire-red and steaming, the hunters
are out the first morning along the edges and

crossings of backroads: guns unlocked hang
broken over their arms: they blow the fist not

caught in the jacket pocket: back home, the wife
is out of the kitchen and off to work, work now

mostly deskwork, women's work: the men pad their
right shoulders, eager for the answering recoil

of the spent thrust: the bark on the snow-paled
trees seems pure male: the brush thicket, the

mazes of stripped vines, the sunk water under
pooled leaves, the slash-back branches are male,

the bucks springing, startled still, dropping:
back at the office, in the shop, the women are

fiddling with papers: out here, the parameters
burst, the deep roots of the caverns spill through.

SPARKLINGS

The mind derives
from the manifold

concretions and
motions of nature

motions of its own
reaching up into the

curvatures of unity
but is not

content to vanish,
extinguished, into the

resolutions of nothingness,
but precisely as the

world's world fades
behind

projects structures of
design,

placements,
so that capability's

entanglements can filigree
the very

freedom of nothingness,
the mind's world

shining direction from
the void of unity

toward the enchantments
of what needs to be.

COOL INTIMACIES

What the power is and what
we can do to save

ourselves with or from it,
how are we to know,

receiving it sieved, in hints
and doubleblips, echoes from

dubious bluffs, silent
declarations, birds and leaves

in motion, announcements
from "bodies" and points of light:

flood or puddle, whatever
it is, it stands

in the Way· we here and
there ride, wade, drown.

FASCICLE

There's a rift of days sunny (not too windy, not
too cold) between leaf- and snowfall when
raking works: away on a weekend, you could

miss it and rain could sog everything slick-flat
or gusts could leave no leaf not lifting
off the ground: stick

around the house, a big sheet ready, a strong-caned
rake strung tight, and catch the sun
just when it stills the air dry: that's likely

to be before some cold front frost-furring
the saw-edged leaves glistened brittle, clouds
tightening the horizon: then the white leaves fly.

LOVING PEOPLE

This enterprise answers
to none of the natural
balances, trade-off's,

exactions: it doesn't
shape to debit
and credit

differences: people are
losing propositions: what
they build flakes away,

even when they don't
take it with them:
no economy of justice,

no sparing, no
payment for services rendered
rolls this circus by:

you make your
mind up first to do it,
rain or shine, giving

or taking: you decide
to decide to love:
then, here and there,

bit by burn, a nod, a
touch, smile, the sweet
love starts showing up.

STANDING LIGHT UP

Thunder grumbles, drops, thuds, breaking
down away (gravel-road rubble) the heads

hidden up in summer haze — and none of the
lightning's veins shows: it could be mountains

lost as much as clouds up there, and the sound
could be of equivalences coming down, avalanches

of stone, mud, snow, not just a front and all-day
soak making up — but so what, anything can be

with a little ink or wine produced: take the
truth that in a drizzle drops tickle leaves so

it's a pause whether it's a breeze: who cares
about a truth like that: nearly all, maybe

all, most truth doesn't matter a tittle of rubble
or rain: what matters is that sometimes the

spirit halts and listens for what outleaps
the insides of summits thunder's rumble has

never jarred: what is to be seen within
brightens the eye brighter than any lightning.

ESTABLISHMENT

To the eye the far ridge's high slopes
are mist, boulders soaked through, blue

floating thin to white, not what the mind
asserts, hard rock skimmed over with brush

the lowering look-alike clouds have to give
to: the mind from the invitations, deceptions

contrives a regularum intervening, the moon,
sun-size, corrected slight: last week I was there

and the brush was trees and the terrain tense roots
rockgrain refused till cracked and felt into.

BROAD BRUSH

To the intricacy of the webbing, oh, good,
here come the broad, coarse, blunt, how
honorable they are, they walk with plunging

casualness, tearing without knowing
through the spun fur of subtlety, and
cyclists put rubber on the road, turn

around and put down more, see who
can put down most, and the farmer plants
fire wild in the fall field's shifty wind and

breathes the smoke with an assurance of
wine bouquet and another farmer mounts the
combine and eats soybean dust for

hours (the phlegm, he says, digests it and
brings it up again) and good lord what room
the round swearer gives the language, he

surrounds the possibilities of elegance, pours
bad beer into the roundness the words fly out
from: I'm tired of honed lines and high

wires and bickering niceties of balance:
disc up an acre by mistake (it was already
seeded) split the rip saw through two or

three grand poplars (tulip leaf and tulip
cone) and let us kick around unsure
and free, legislation so much milkweed silk.

FIRST COLD

Well, the white asters
are wide open (there's
even a chicory
blossom or two
left on a big weed)

but it's too cold
for the bees to come:
every now and then
a snowflake
streaks

out of the hanging gray,
winter's first whitening:
white on white let it be,
then, flake
to petal — to hold for a

minute or so: meanwhile,
golden bees are milling at
the door, to pour
out should that other
gold, the sun, break in.

REGARDS REGARDLESS

We had something to do for a moment
with the eternity of things, we made
contact, the sweeps deeper than we

knew, moving in and out without regard,
we, bits, too little too brief to take
the awful informings in: age edges

us aside: we vacate offices (such as
listening for the loud, dull oriole
in May) to others whose earth earth's

becoming: but, aside, we note clearly,
having them separate again, bit from
power, second from time's springs:

look, there goes eternity, still astir:
here are roses seen before: nothing's
to save us at last save loss itself:

even our gatherings, bits and pieces,
will with our central dissolving float
free, disordered, unaligned, the chairs

empty, our voices in none of the rooms:
well, it was enough, even if nothing
came of it, no, it was something even

if it becomes nothing, the show turned
full round: freedom freely
enough allowed burns free, burns us free.

THE TIME RATE OF CHANGE

You mosey around, idling here and
there for years,
unaware that a waiting is hanging

out for you, and then one day
you feel a light hindrance
like a floating, cut-away spider web

touch your shoulder: and some
years later, perhaps, another,
still light but with a smallish

tug to it, and then one day you
trip and catch in an entanglement like
direction, but the direction is

rope-loose and you don't mind that
much: more years and a fine halter
of dense constraints bites in,

and a kind of speed breaks out,
not just speed but acceleration, and
you begin to look back and also,

and with equal alarm, forward,
and the speed picks up, the direction
narrows, and the speed is light's.

GREETING VERSES

What do I find right at the center of my interpersonal
relationships: a slightly dispersed but indisputably
tinctured core of brutality: go to the hospital

the question is not whether your life is at stake
but whether you can pay the bill, guaranteeing it on
admission (or no admission) and proving it (or not getting

out) on release (if any): this bit of realism
clutches our floating values underneath like a bracket
under a bouquet: if someone pauses to

congratulate me on some slight nothing, I see the
quiver of a curse undermine his lip: he
tries to make a better world even while it crumbles in

on him and us (a brutality): when I give my body to another
(or take another's) I sometimes fear more
body being taken than was offered, an overextension

of contract: hearts and flowers, scented sentiment, garden
varieties greet us, how lost we want to be in fictions and
fabrications: a worm cores this world's doings, look out.

MIND STONE

This stricture produces now and then a flash of castles,
bodies of another sort, foreign and opposite, their
shuddering airiness native though in a sense to

their origin: balloons in inexperienced hands worry
me; I stagger   ─ of loss when they nod upward
loose: having   taying on the ground, I've talked

pieces of it ir   ing off: if I dwell surprisingly
on ashes, sha   into death, it's to keep
the colors dc   ing glass-white mountings to the

blue bottom   s, at least, going out to watch the
canopies of   down like dust by the unlimited
particles of (h, yes, it hasn't been easy — blue

bright-open   rly radiant, severe scythes burning me
off the tops__   iciling opposites, one grab in turf, say,
the other in space, promotes perilously extravagant shows.

DOWNING LINES

This morning it was
as if the spruce
stood in a sea

the wind rocked
it so (the wind-sea
sounded like a

sea-wind)
leaning it
way over with

lengthy insistencies, too;
the ground wobbled, roots rising
and waving — even, I

thought, even trees
stand the test
of standing,

lone trees' risk
unbroken by other trees,
grove trees, though,

skinned with rattling
and rubbing —
even the spruce finds

the middle way
between taking on and
keeping up, the

wind's abrasions, scourings
making a show of
difference with solid ground.

WHITEWATER

They say the time of the individual's past: oh,
well: again: you become more quirky and put
a word in that touches on irrelevance — *flimsy*:

rapids warn you way off they're coming up: you hear
them down or up the canyon: you pull ashore
and trek to see what

shipbottom's in for or what portage will entail:
squalls, too, give notice, sometimes
short, at sea, a surge loosening through dead air:

the guy ahead, picking off the earliest edges of
indication, has an advance on knowing but endures
longer the windup of the onsweep: it may be better

to waken in tangling's final concision and resolution,
death or surprise your summary welcome and dismissive
look: but if portage is to do it must do thought out.

ERMINOIS

The weatherman says "if
the rain continues the roads
will be icy tonight":
of course, but what if it
doesn't: or,

"if the spoken language lay
down and turned up its toes,
the written language
would have its balls": well,
sure: or, "if word order

meant nothing in this language . . ."
but it does:
there is forward being
in being, a resource
unsurroundable, a living

giving forth, so
treasurable one dwells there
in the tiny place saying,
yes, barely, to
the life that is and is to be.

CONSTRUING DECONSTRUCTION

The showboat, the main sway of the motion,
rounds the downbend in a toot-white scream-plume,
and there are all the fluffy couples out

strolling the floating parquets and palisades,
parasols aflutter as flamingoes' pink airs,
and spit-smart bells peal and bang with agreed

on significances, and here's the dockside
welcoming committee dressed up to endorse mutual
expectations: meanwhile, those rope-servant or

misaligned few who can't or won't know polish &
candy-striped jackets & crystalline sweet-sips
watch the oilslick spin through kitchen slicks,

behold the silver flicks of mudchurned fry, the
gouging out of plankton habitats by the sternwheel's
stalling back washes, dumped garbage grinding under.

ELITE STREET

The devil in me is, I think, among the divines:
defining myself out of the camp of the blessed,
I've paraded right in, becoming knowledgeable

about the robes, slippers, the clever absence of heat,
the rosy tinges of near concern on lips and cheeks,
the halo sizes, numbers, and, probably, colors, too,

and astonished by the airy sprinkling of habitation,
a camp only being in the right could defend: I'm a
natural for training in the doings of indolence,

idle idolatry, and for jiving the best rap around:
these divines, so changed, so turned out, I suspect,
must have been, my style, demons first, who else

could have figured things out so precisely, to set up:
I have the energy for this kind of aspiration,
and this is the club I've long been meaning to join.

GOOD MORNING, THIS MORNING

Death is very common but not,
I hear, 100% effective; one,

once, unjustly, I suppose, hung
up, downed, rose, a rising

that delivered death to plenitudes
in scatterings, swingings, stakes

of grubbed up flesh (set afire),
limbs, heads cut off, etc.: is

this a small price to pay for
something to believe in: nature

is just here, a lovely if careless
spread, and its dynamics, seen

to and smoothed out, can be
suggestive: otherwise, the fridge's

clean but for what we ourselves
devise: belief, at any cost,

serves life: let life do without.

WALKING SONG

A little shower
and, the
sun come out,

ditch-bottom
brilliance
blinds you:

the highest, doubling
deep,
companions with

the lowest and the
lowest
spins up to

heights you
can't
bear to witness.

SENTIMENT

All things that live die but even
rivers dry up or roll
out of their beds and rising lands

sometimes remove seas and ranges
snow tops all year wear down eventually:
the earth, of course, itself came

into being and must in time be cindered:
think of the shock, though, meanwhile,
of the minor changes, a friend in an

accident, being late to your son's
soccer match, a leaning tree in a
yard an old house has moved away from.

ANXIETY'S PROSODY

Anxiety clears meat chunks out of the stew, carrots, takes
the skimmer to floats of greasy globules and with cheesecloth

filters the broth, looking for the transparent, the colorless
essential, the unbeginning and unending of consommé: the

open anxiety breezes through thick conceits, surface congestions
(it likes metaphors deep-lying, out of sight, their airs misting

up into, lighting up consciousness, unidentifiable presences),
it distills consonance and assonance, glottal thickets, brush

clusters, it thins the rhythms, rushing into longish gaits, more
distance in less material time: it hates clots, its stump-fires

level fields: patience and calm define borders and boundaries,
hedgerows, and sharp whirls: anxiety burns instrumentation

matterless, assimilates music into motion, sketches the high
suasive turnings, skirts mild natures' tangled, nubby clumps.

THE LAND OF THE
KNOBBLE-JOBBLE TREE

A shaded branch will through etiolation stretch, even though it has
little sun to stretch with, to get into the sun, and a sunny branch
will, having resources, put on length: for these two reasons, bushes

tend to get bigger: trees that do this, too, are not more scientific
than other trees, just bigger: although, since all trees and bushes
react this way, I suppose they're all bigger together, a uniformity of

effect and a limitation of means so egalitarian as to be totalitarian,
a political reading: bushes willing to be small are rare: more often
than not, small bushes have not found a way to get bigger: there's

burning drought to hold back for or a winter that lashes everything even
with ice or there are dunes it's more important for roots to grow down
into than branches up from: things small are unwillingly small, unless

like animalcules of water droplets they're too small to dream in or toward
a more noticeable dimension: things small when stirred take the vertical
too quickly, standing not fifteen degrees leant off true, whereas weightier

membes level a kind of solemn directness at you, a bigger thrill, though,
than the trivial alert: some branches, shaded or sunny, don't grow mea-
surably however often they stiffen into and out of reach: some sizable and

very considerable things widen and lengthen in a single plane, broaden
like a leaf, open and close, furl and foment in organizations by groove
or lamina, outright astonishments: some like a small bush, some scanty:

some short-cropped, some moss-like long: some like a curled, I suppose,
bush: or wavy: some care only for the secrets thick bushes keep away
or open to: some cut down all their bushes to a lush-lawn prickleness

and manifest everything they have openly: a thing is not insignificant
just because you say it is insignificant, nor empty just because you say
it is empty, and a thing is not meaningless just because you say so,

nor absurd: you must make a thing whatever it is and having made it so
it must always be what it is and not the thing it isn't that you didn't
make: this positive procedural edge, though, cuts both ways: a pile of

meanings is meaningless, whereas an emptiness of meanings has not been
created empty, and if you try to create it empty you will get something
in it: existence is an unavoidable fact, and there is nothing else —

"nothing" — except existence: there is much surdity but no ab, none, not
a hairpiece: there are, for example, different colored bushes and many can
be dyed: a world of bedeckings and fragrances, kinky, ribbony, floral.

CAPABILITIES

Can nature form a rule ruling nature
out, a line differential to the point
materiality loses its fuzzy-fine edges

describing it: not the knots, balances,
compensations, quandaries, divisions,
paradoxes, not those big centralities

that leave a little somewhere to go
when going uses itself up, but (everything
settled, believe me) tiny errors of

curvature, shades of misfitting, leftover
hues the colors didn't take — there
attention flares up like a rabbit

shot: can we go on being entertained
by the large matters (not we
oldies): the wild, the exceptional

break new waves through: nature
may draw the line of our own and its own
vanishing: still, we're here where

such states of being (love?) occur now
and then we can't put our minds on nature's
own doings, and we dwell in reveries of

adequate spirit nature may not know how
to float, surpass, or continue in:
remarkable sucked fizzy drinks burning the mucous.

MINUTIAL IMPRESS

Nothing will ever be the same again, he said,
not even the same will be the same again,
the same itself acquiring through time
the promotion of shift-small differences:

still, is will be is, we know, close
to it, close to forever: and anything
worked off or away into perfection
will be subtracted from the coming round

of the next coming round: so, not too
much perfection, and even that the kind
near perfection, what can fall back and
help stir the confusion and élan: but

even though is will be is (a form of the
highest patience and knowing) even the
biggest is, returning, plays out through
history extraordinary ragged changes:

should we wish not to get it straight, since
to do so is to vanish into nothing,
nothing vanished perhaps except vanishing itself:
a little here & there into is: the rest churns.

SHOWUPS

Never to be the fool, I always play the fool, but
ready ever to be an even greater fool, sometimes
fail the role and make never sometimes, indeed,

alas: the sobriety of headhung
humiliation when the heart offers itself up
to sacrifice, the goddess clicking away on

cobblestones from some gray dead end, the wall flat,
a stoppage, blank as the wailing spaces of lost
mind: then I, fool's fool, the true show folded,

test technique again beyond willing, easy
failure to see with what colorations imagination
twists the other side of waste; the fool's

fool dies and the play re-opens, grief-wrenched
hair fabulous and startled, pants over-heisted,
face jacked up a millimeter or so above true.

MODES AGAINST TOO MUCH

My poems, if poems
other than casual
entrances into systems, are

lulls by which
motion going by too
fast as in damaging winds

slows to assume
(forced into the definition of)
mediating rhythms,

sketchy but entangling
knots, in this
wind tight patterns

obstructive and unyielding
likely to come down
or be hauled off whole,

criss-cross trellises
in typhoon, say:
but bits, strings,

swerving (lessening and
swelling) elongations
that giving to

the wind like high water or
sails catch a part
of it formed into known
ways, let go, withstood.

SKY RIDES

My constructions aim so far
or high away, they get me

'out of myself' as they must for
my sight to build a site:

but out of myself, I rise into
alignment with others' far

projections and there we all are,
stripped of earthly material,

the knots we build from, but
safely together, as luminous

as we would have been, born
into a luminous place: but,

it's the way it goes, we fall
back at times, singled out again,

into the dense knowledge of
the word or two we can't,

shouldn't, or won't say that said
could get us about okay on the ground.

HEIGHTS KNOWN

Love surgent, equipped with the direction
of sail, is matchless, the heading right on in
through the weather, ups and downs, the high
swipes and weltering, but afterwards there is
the not-so-spanking hull flat in doldrums
oblivious as absence, and there is the possibility
of tides elsewhere, of coves and offshore
anchorages, island-scented breezes: and in love
the planks steam and split or a small fire
finds its way up a hatch or timbers peel and
time-consuming decisions have to be made:
love's bells loll and clang these storms and calms
averaging out into a kind of indifference one
luckily doesn't assume in the first place and go by.

CONSERVATIONIST

Little time left to work with,
the old say, is like youth's having
worked with little: birth's center

spent's soon the sinkhole's
oozing intake: who though (if not
the old and long-accustomed) will

care for the old: not the old and
long-accustomed, imminent deliverance
from new and old their watchwords:

the child, coming into so much
time to fill, shape, name,
the child's the keeper, traditionalist.

A LITTLE THING LIKE THAT

life comes under no other
propositions than mountain decrees,

it seems at times;
seldom if a meander is allowed

can one see it far: it bends
away with its willows

behind a boulder-head or sheer face-off:
winding is the way of life

I would choose, would you, if
I could choose, for I would

like always to be on the other side
of wherever there's trouble

or pointing responsibility
or too much nailing down: just the

flexibility of brooks, dribbling over
stones or swelling up to dribble

over stones: I have always felt,
as one should, I think, shy

of mountains: they don't seem like
breasts to me —

             but they rise
up august into air-starving presences

and they command views: I like
to swerve away from commands

because I'm unconvinced that I could
do all the things I might

be commanded to do or that I would
want to do them, and I would rather

feint a dissolve into a curvature,
a curvature of disappearance, as

around a hill or down from a rise:
may I not feel the speech of mountains

when they "speak" and may I wander
with meanders, not seeing far (ahead

or behind) and picking up willows
wherever possible, or alders and

stopping to have lunch in the shade
and drink from boulder-drained melts.

GETTING ABOUT

The windiest morning this
year (the second month) bringing
the first warm
heave of rain from the south:

starlings, this ocean's
winter schools, knot
close, thickening twig-mesh
in broad oaks and hold

fast, clasped to the boiling sways:
flare-winged crows
flap, tossed backwards, dip into penetrating
spills to check the wind:

a hawk, though, tilting,
splits wings-in directly ahead into the
blundering wall, loosening its
stones like silt.

DECEMBER STARLINGS

A sheer loops in and berries bead
the oak's sticky lofts: twittering
blooms a dense stippling, a burn

that eases off with settling, but
just then before dusk's blurs,
a loaded twig snaps and the whole

sheet ripples in report;
the black sheer unfurls and swirls
away to fold into night elsewhere.

STRINGS

for Don Randel

The yellow house
of the willow is
threadbare, now,

the shiny little shingles
missing,
thick as thatch

under the snow floor the
wind's laid in:
inside and outside

glare nearly the same
cold and light:
what is that

black rill
taking away — bits of
summer dark, bark

shadow, scrimps
of fern shade from
den holes;

it's draining banks
and mounds white,
churning

narrows and dropping
away
quickly down

shale-shelves:
the crisp of my steps
in dry snow is

the "shine" of
stone underground:
I'm so happy!

the house nearly
gone, so is
the grief,

and yet
a wind-frail house
is here.

WINDING UP

The sun's risings and
settings on the west
ridge like
an accordion swell

and shrink the year's
music, a music rolling
too quick now to step to —
we rocking on the waves,

the frequency working up
shaking the underload:
soon the hum-burr will start,
grind us free of the ground,

loop loose from the tip
of the sharpest sine peak,
a point, catapult
to the long way away.

MIDDLING SEASONS

The weather here hits so many extremes the
transitions sweep moderation: this morning
ninety mile an hour gusts strip live

wood from the maple crowns and on the ground
bend whatever bends over over, root-eruptions,
scatterings, whole
activations of leaves, bark, twigs,

plastic foam, sheet — scurryings, unwindings
blustered up: this winter stalled to
the deepest chill ever: last winter was the

coldest span: the year before, the most snow:
then the highest temperature, and the highest
ever sustained, in a blocked inversion

two weeks long: high water: drought: scientists
blame sunspots: others say, in spite
of the centenary figures, it was never any different:
a few ask how much quietude we wished: well, I

need a skinny place in there not a statistical moderation,
really moderate, a sunny calm clime in which to hang
onto some wrong idea about the nature of things.

LOOKING WAY OFF

The winter day after days
of lows and flurries
and one trench of snow
cleared brilliantly and I

went to the window to see
the sun, striking through
everything from blue spruce
to black rose-branch

to the tops of gold burdock,
touch down on the ridge,
the clarity, the line,
the dazzling dalliance and

surprising myself said,
"Make me right," but tightened
airless till, till I imagined
from on high an unassenting

reply, "You're right wrong."
so I cleave to my holding.

OBSESSION

The wordwhirl stood
high in my head
so many

years dustdevil-like
it dominated
the ridges and

ranges of whatever else
was there, so
that now,

the whirl worn
low, wobbled
diminished

out of sight behind
a stone, I
think what has

become of the way
things were, the
ridges empty, too.

ANGER TANGLE

The world (that
approves his
art) would (if it
knew him)

condemn his self,
a contempt he
answers with anger
which (since

it is futile)
turns to lassitude,
indifference,
dejection but

a contempt
(strait-laced, fat-faced)
he finds
contemptible until

he, generous,
understands the world's
contempt to absolve
his own,

which understanding
though takes
implication into his
self, self-despising,

to which he
reacts with anger or
indifference
and loss of self.

THE DEEP SLOW

The pheasant's skinny
feet skid
on ice freezing
rain polished
the snow with last night
and around the round
birdfeeder's tin roof

a carousel of icicles drops
part way
nearly shutting the birds out:
heaviness heavier
than leaves glazes
bush and branch,
the hemlocks withered

old men come up from lakebottom:
if the clouds weren't
easing along oozing occasional
bright edges,
this could be
the condition
the world had settled on.

SAYING SAYING AWAY

The point of a poem is to become wordless, to find
the rounding out that assimilates reductiveness and
assertion to an unspeakable whole: the end of the poem
is to reconstruct silence, a cure of words, to subvert
the fragmentary, discursive, partial, definitional

into stance and feeling: when the stance of a poem becomes
whole and still, its motions are like travels of light
and surface through the aspects of a piece of sculpture:
no act of analysis sees the whole at once: the poem
reconciles, ends, and holds its motions: its images

lose their sharp edges and colors into the tones and
moods of landscape, into the inexhaustible suggestiveness
of impressionism: the end of a poem is to lose itself
in itself, to give over the partialities of rhythm,
image, and sense to coherences words can give no access

to and have no access to, a place where the distinction
between meaning and being is erased into the meaning of
being: what a poem says may be its least and most
misleading ploy: how it holds its behavior opens the poem
up to indefinableness and inexhaustibility, ontology

and teleology become one, to the focused point where in
mulling over and meditating on the poem we can sort
out its behavior and ours and define for ourselves what
we like and don't and return our definitions to criticism
and instruction, idling, and waking nonchalance.

LINE DRAWINGS

The pear leaf blister mite should be
compelled to stay off pear leaves
(how can the leaves fill out to produce

the branch weight of fruit coming — the
fruit already set up by snow-chunks of
blossoms blown — and how can

the blistered leaves do the solar-panel
work, taking up the collections, that
changes light wooden: you know

how soon pear wood mellows and falls
off the trees) I wonder if the pear leaf
blister mite might not be suitable for

peach leaves where the wood's harder
or, no, should they be moved
to the big patches of that bamboo-like

import, the smooth, heart-shaped leaves,
detestable tall weeds you can't get
rid of because of runners underground

that shoot shoots up everywhere:
why can't the pear leaf blister mites
prefer something despicable and

eradicate it and leave the pears alone
that are shaped just like women, the
narrow-shouldered stem end and the round

ampling of the other: why must we
put up with this equation where anything
good for anything is

answered by a tantamount negative: how
the pear leaf blister mites would react
to these quarrels and postulations, who

knows, but what are we here for, to figure
out every little thing or to clear
a place off for whatever we have to say?

PREY

The old man in a shimmy, his arms
blotched bruises, inches barefoot
down the hall, his head ticking

in the deep stoop:
the orderly, slowed behind,
too many tasks ahead, swoops

the old man up in his arms,
and the little old man flies,
astonished as a stricken bird:

at the radial desk, centralizing
the wings, the nurses look on
the bright side not to see too much.

VERY HIGH CONDITION

The long ridge
line (winter's
sunrise-sunset
scale) of
stone and sky holds
hill sweeps, passes —
indifferent to our
settlement here:
I look at it and
mean nothing: yet
near the center
central indifference,
neither pardon nor
indictment,
runs: I need forgiveness
for wrongs inadvertent
and not, known to
me and not:
but there's the ridge
line, recourse, an
assumption beyond
rescue and fall, a
purity we can
note, only note.

THE CATEGORY OF LAST RESORT

for Louise and Tom Gossett

The least criticism, at least the least
insistent (though in a way a
very big affair) signals untold (if

it's really there) from the well center
of indifference, nature's best preserved,
most essential bailiwick: how

sweet it is to move out, how easing,
from the strictures, penalties, binds
of choice and difference to the

bluet-sprinkled meadow's
hedged-in, willy-nilly brook and on up
along the rise to the high woods,

the unfolding and falling away into distance!
not so much because the brook's
careless whether one wades or

leaps it, or strolls by disregarding its
trinkling glass, and not because the day is
so clear one can hardly see it — the day! —

if only one could pick something, something
distilled from the branch-high air of
a tulip poplar just leafing, and gulp

it down, desire's patent, purest possibility
and sweetest prize, so as to secure
oneself against the unraveling

of a mislived or unlived life, the whole
caught complete in a take: but
I hope there's an alternative, an

indifference indifferent to its own indifference,
a center the reading of all our
differences into would not stain or

sway, a place any difference could come to to
weigh itself in, a judge (perhaps
missing from her seat) whose attention yelling

logic could not attract: there, though,
listening for his sentence,
one could play

every fact of difference and desire into action
and, hearing nothing, find in nothing
the nearest satisfaction to being everything.

THE CLENCHED-JAW SCHOOL

The holdout of brook-glitter in a drought,
the skittery edginess of leaves against a windy hedge row —

I sit out of the way by the brookfalls
looking in places too drab for pilgrimage
for revelations such
as the sun's surviving the all-day splintering
of running water, the

water broken, too, over and over into falls: stones hear
or say my verses:
brookbanks set out
staves of music for me:
I put the bars in, I take them out, I move them around.

CEPPAGNA

The heights, fastnesses, are sharp and
wild: olive trees scatter into the open,
die out, and, beyond,
higher, dandelions sweeten

thin air: sheep go up where spring
grass winters into hay: there the
black bear runs and knows
a way old as rocks: the wolf, crisp

with practices, whirls, and the moon
burns his eyes: when the shepherd,
his third week, runs out of food, he is,
except for greens, out — homeless,

wineless, lampless, wifeless:
his eyes feed lean on
the liquor of stars, and just gravity
gets him back to earthly hungers.

PIT LINES

The grave, though, though it ends
so much recollection, ends less
than a life, whole stages, as of theaters,
having been blocked out by scenery or,
earlier, locked away, fields that got

no further than design or that, opened
to the light once, folded, possibilities
having slimmed untoward way before the end:
in fact, sometimes, abundance or no
abundance (not white paint for a mountain

cone), the flimsiest remnant, a scrap
of bridal veil or a pocketwatch fob,
makes it to the grave, surrender
after surrender having mowed down the fields
and worn out the stagehands: laughter,

preventing, brings tears: graves are
gleaned and filled: but the wind does
not enter in: it deserts the body and
the grave and stays gone: the hills aren't
indifferent, they are too neutral for this.

SILVERING SHADOW

The frail-green woods bubble and peep, goldfinches
thickening the branch-splayed heights.

an early day version of the night peepers,
not here yet: spring is here: warmer by the paling

fence where the thousand-legger, dug up with the dandelion
root, panics in the light: but nearly too cool

in the open when lakewind sheets up over the lawn's
swell: with so much burgeoning to gather force,

the bulgings and oozings of cancer wards, the girl
stricken responsible after generous sex, estrange:

splendor has the scariest shade:
in hell, the word-one picks out a heavenly word.

ABSCISSION

The flow-finding of the making impulse
rounds the curves of what-is
and shakes out scaffolding
suitable to the outline of the perception

and so on and under the severest skepticism
takes in colors, flavors,
the characters of whole things (of whatever scale,
a circle of curve assuming the magnitude)

as belonging to universes of their own
proprieties — and so the making
gathers into the disintegrating and integrating
motions of its dispositional axis

until, having fulfilled its time, having searched
out its completion, it scores the fissure that
cracks it off while it can be saved,
and it becomes different and timeless.

MICROINSCRIPTIONS

The fall of deep-bottom arctic water down
the Atlantic midrib, a glacial inch a
month, the high assimilations of the free-wandering

jet stream, these places we look to for durance
or dwelling motion — sometimes, ephemeral, we need
them so much (or the floating apart of continents,

a centimeter a year, into the lank voyages) we
forget the many shimmering little absolute
disappearances, goings-away like local problems

solved (a drowned nest floated free) whereas the big
problems dwell in unsolvability's sway, useful
as systems of lasting definition, too big to be

let go of, currencies: everything is saved in the
disappearances and returns except what we like, the
particular melt of light in a particular

eye, that is the construct whose fire is so nearly
inexpressible we think the thinnest, highest
meanders of ozone not so crushing: what, completely

away, however much is left where so much — lakes,
clouds — flows without loss, oh, well, though lakes
and clouds can't keep either: and, of course, the

axis has shifted more than once and Arctic migrated
down and around, and the jet stream, before oxygen,
bore a different bole: all's lost — there is an

ultimate mere celestial glow not much having to
do with our business, though the energy base of
any business: still, and specially since we stay

so many blinks, the caresses of hands and lips
having to do at times with young ones or at some time
trying to share final pain — there we hold on.

READINGS BY WAYS

The epicurean (and stoic) philosophers,
monists and
dualists,

are interesting (they show
that time over time
unwinds nearly the same story) but

how can I resist the creek,
slowing over depth
or breaking into shiny ramshackles

on a rise of pebbles or blurring
storm history in weed-slants
along high banks: I get

caught up in clouds illustrating
the sky or muddying out: I can't
get enough of the nodding

adjustment when a
squirrel leaps on or off a branch,
the trail quaking: still, I

like it when the old philosopher says
live unknown, whole
histories like unread creeks.

ABANDON

The crows during
warm fall spells
work their way up

whatever direction
the wind will be coming from
the next windy day

so they can bound downslope
cawing long surprises, dipping at
one another, folding their

wings and like splendid
trash skimming the woods:
when it's gold and red

and windy and they fall out
of the north, the exhilaration
appears

never to have been earned and they
seem to take the fall for
the only kind, the only one.

LOCAL ANTIQUITIES

The brook, older
than manuscripts, tells
the news:

the hills, out in the
rain,
antedate altars:

when the painter turns
from "absolute"
paint, it begins to

crack: weeds and
bushes
where cities stood

put the rubble
down: we
separate

our things from
things, but only
changing with change

stays beyond things
and us, mocks change's
mocking changes.

CHANGING STATIONS

The all-night rain running
off and soaking through
into the narrows
tore up the brooks, leaned

slates of shale
against the banks and, cutting some
bank away, rearranged chip shale
into new mounds, tiled close,

as if by hand, by
water mortar (what a sound) but now
the brook's so still,
pane clear, a treetop scrap of

birds like stubborn leaves
shines shaking in the brookbed
filled
with a deeper ditch of sky.

COLLAPSED STRUCTURES

Terror when it goes leaves lifelessness's big hole:
one does not wish it back, terror, fierce inhabitant,
a guest abruptly returned from a delayed leaving
there again at the door
so the doorways stir and fly: but how

great the vacancy! the attention turning
about to no attendant, the polish of absence's
gist: there's the first-quarter moon,
though, its own light emptying out the whole
dome, the sight of its loneliness confirming

one's own: just somewhere to look
as if to find absence all together in one place:
recalling terror, though, may not be the same
as terror really gone, for in the recall of
suasions of the recently departed is still much

to muse on, the bridgeways and slidings to relief,
the simmering into assimilation of humiliation
and demand, the guest's needs now only
images not to be answered or answered to:
if terror moves on away through the miles and

hours and relief loses focus, tires of dawdling,
and feels the first scorch of nothingness, oh, then,
emptiness's own terror becomes another guest or
the same or just another some day, after
long entertainments, to take grateful leave of.

FLAT ROCK

Streams divided (around a boulder-cluster or
barge) heal right back together:

gravity's bed takes it all one way, the same
water the substance of distant, subsequent

occasions: water shaken white over
rapids-stones downstream bursts white again

into falls-holes, a permanent eventuum
that takes a name — falls, of course, but

Blank Falls if people stare there, and
this water wrinkles later on through a

sluice so fast people stop to think
about it: Streaking Sluice names that place:

later still this stream spreads out flat over
a shallows-wide ledge-bed, a swim you can
get all the way into almost without getting wet.

FLURRIES

Streaks, drifts, mounds
of meaning build,
flare: roof-lochs spill,

catching at the eaves
meanings
icicle-clear:

glaciers grind visionary
meanings down nordic gorges,
letting fall

rivers to rustle
narrows amply clean cut:
hold still, the

spirit cries, hold this,
but motion
undermines meaning with meaning.

THE DEEP END

Stillness can't hold
still, gets
the shivers and shatters:

self-regulating systems
swinging through opposing
loops' ceaseless adjustment

and re-direction, though, find
variable ways to stay:
mood sweeps, so long as no

immoderation tears them
loose, bar off a middle ground
for ordinary happiness's

strawberry plants, say (subject
to frost), whereas no body
bears (can it?) the hum of

undeviating happiness any
more than a constancy of
blithe cold: ups and downs

work out a way of showing up
from down as well as an
interregnum of nonchalance:

I'm impressed with the way
things work, work
itself setting up mid-regions

of rest, whereas (again) rest,
what can become of rest,
more rest?, so much rest

edging restlessness up: if
I were to make a moral
of this, I'd say that

if you have something to go
along with, go along with
it, because millions of goings

and comings before us have
smoothed and ruffled balancing
grooves, the groove itself,

so hard to find, a turning
back of going in — a puzzlingly
remarkable territory to greet.

REASONING POWER

Sometime between thaws, blows, and freezes,
a sawtoothed leaf became seamlessly sealed
in ice but now, a long thaw underway, it lies

disclosed on the surface, surface having
inched in to it: who's to say as I tell you
this that the brookful of ice, honeycombed

with lattices, worked sucked-through with
holes that underspin overpouring and downchurning
water is going on with its work and that I

am holding alone here looking at held leaves
and lattices for a reason: do I need
reason to tell the reason: would one wandering

this way be dwelling in the strong offices of
reason or would he, nonreasoning, be looking
for the indifference of the sawtooth edge that

softens as it gets out of ice and dries brittle
in a wind that shows it a new home, dissolution
its destination: merely, merely, merely naked

in the shrunken spine turned away from rejection:
does one need to say that in the abundance
of nothing a leaf surprises the mind full of

design, bilateral symmetry in asymmetry, that
these minds unoccupied with the given hold such
starvations of emptiness available, any bit of

> action, a leaf turning
> over in the wind,
> can become what is.

TENACITIES

Shrinking back for coherence's holding
gauge, closing in, we
came not to dust but to

a mode or condition, nothingness,
where smallness, looked into, grew vast:
we found the beam the mind

construes between nothing and nothing,
from which it seems intolerable to move
either way: we said must we

give up the hope of forms not yet seen:
we stepped back out into the open where
roses blacken in sleet or, given up too far, spill apart.

BLUES IN THE VALLEY

Route 96B has lain over there
bending up and away over the
ridge on its way out,
going out day and night,

while I've been here valley-bound
31 years and got so
I think I can hear
singing in the rocks, riffles,

the cool dream-reels
of boulders:
light bands near sundown
break out

underpinning the clouds on west hill,
and I know how
they've looked before, may look again,
how they'll thin down and fine away.

PACKAGING

Roll
up the edges of
the squared-off, flattened-out,
two-dimensional
mind,

pull the corners up and tie them
off at the top,
a sphere or bag, so that
anyone thinking
will

have to think about more sides
at once than one,
get volume
within his
definitions,

and become less secure
that summer with him is
summer everywhere,
his ice cap feeling's
only leaning.

SERPENT COUNTRY

Rolled off a side of mountains or
hills, bottomed
out in flatland but getting

away, winding,
will be found a
scale-bright snake — brook, stream, or river, or,

in sparest gatherings,
a wash of stones or a green
streak of chaparral across sand.

EARLY STONES

Returning from the thawed creek
and winter-hungry for early
slugs or mole crickets, he
turns a stone on
the clear-woods floor, thinks to
pick it up, steadying his pace
back to the cave porch where
he drops it,
an investment against the fireless
summer nights when the tiger
moves too near in, hard to scare.

CONNECTING MISSES

Pursue a subject, it flares
into division,
branches raveling, blurring
off, networks splitting
ramification till
splintering fines: or
some mountain, perhaps,
offering a tunnel with little view,

interrupts, straightening the
lessening: still,
no matter
how slight, subjects
get whole attentions
to be in: when
the subject runs out leaving
everything oceanic and still

undone will the world have
disappeared, too, or
will we light out
across sea-swings, savannahs,
brambles, woodlots,
with a clear line that
cuts a new subject free to a
world's pursuing?

TENURE'S PLEASURES

Plenty of the young dropped
this morning when the rain

iced a quarter inch jewel-hard
on the walkways,

but the supple young rose
(and some dropped and rose again)
unharmed:

here and there an old professor,
though, hit the pack and as

he stirred files rattled in insurance
suites and big money moved

dangerously: fortunately, far
off in Michigan, a plane's
wings iced over, too, and

the novelist scheduled to
read here this afternoon

canceled and now, so wonderful
the variety of possibility,

we can all go on home early
to liniment our bruises or watch
the fissures swell — it's swell.

PRESSING ON

Over the rise they find significance behind
them, and the significance of coming down

even again next to nothing: love was the deep
valuable now buried under the rise memory can

hardly plunder to resurrect, at times, and
given the pains of closing out ahead, a kind

of floating eases through; they have no
reality to settle to worthwhile: but free

enough to float! the work done, the children
schooled, the mortgage burned, long-term

insurance in place: the blood of memory thins,
pain shears entanglements away, the floating

ranges out becoming dreams: when they try to touch
down the ground under them flows.

THE STORY

Oblivion keeps the caterpillar bright.

PERIOD

One gets started
conditionally perhaps
or
introductorily
and after
a ceremony or so of
pause and
preparation
rises into the main
business,
strikes a couple
of dashing heights —
breathless —
followed by
parentheses picking
up and holding
back
but then drops
a semicolon
(giving serious
notice); but
coordinating away,
though, as if
into a new beginning,
tensions knitting
newly into rise,
ramification
and wandering having
blurred

outcome, when closure
arrives as
usual punctual
with a rest.

THE WAY OF ONE'S DESIRE

One not lost finds no way:
terror brightens what it sees:
home's a destination one

departs with to part with:
okay never looks to be okay,
and not-okay, looking, sees

the only not-okay: you who
know, even as if not knowing,
tell me, how does one err

to find one's erring: where
in the wild are the wiles
that school the way back home?

HURRICANE

Migrating along (butterfly-like,
actually) I came on
a sweeping system, round

and big, and traveling with it
forgot it was not
I (a magnificent loss for that

much gain) but the system played
out in time, dissipating
into severally estranged

motions and, an edged-out
peripheral bit myself, I dropped
dashed to a breaking

shoal and fluttered bedazzled
with separation
but also with — what a relief.

THE CRYSTAL TREE

May we tinker with nature, define &
adopt, adjust her procedures, till
we can make a nature

that unwinds us at last from
the coils of nature: but
giving ourselves over in the

admiration of study, measuring
the delicacies of balance,
the fineries of difference,

how may we get free enough
not to think ourselves
sacrilegious in overturning

dynamisms so spelled out
into spellings of our own
slightly askew: some of us

may study and admire, even praise,
perhaps, while others assume
the lofty scantlings of

arrogance and twist
the workings our way, forcing
our ends: and our ends, that

we may not die, or that we
may build what keeping itself
perfect cannot die, glass

intelligences freed at last
to roam immortal ranges
out there: not to die,

this the will arisen on an orb's skin
where death's transmission's
nearest absolute, a

single victory from it our
widest claim: but if it is
not the end of matter to make

good people or people good,
we may envision the fierce
laying nature waste

that brought death in
and we may conquer and
rebuild till nature,

against itself, supports
the eternal life it
never would allow, though

it let the will arise,
disguised and mute at first,
then bespoken as by one

exceeding his standing,
varying his way,
commanding: this one

is coming up among us, his
demand answering,
to balance our fall,

even if to the end of
the human,
beginning another unknown.

A PRETTY LOOKING SIGHT

I suppose we must act as if —
though some old man
is turning windless in a room —
language is too strict

to pay a visit,
to slouch loose out of tense indifference
and go over there
and say something to the old man

or for him:
after all, pretty soon he
won't be winded anymore:
then where would poetry be

with no place to go
calling: but if it doesn't
go through one mouth, enter
ears, and go out some other

mouth, how will it keep
rigorous, straitened up
into shape: oh, well, real
height, carelessness, mounts so

sharply up words probably
strip out
of its wires and the wires,
climbing, probably

melt to light, and at the pinnacle
where this world could be stood
is a sort of place, highly
designated, and empty.

FOCUS

Fellow down the street
(it's like flocculation)
throws a party and

Cadillacs (and
a Mark Continental or
so) assemble

lining all eight sides
of the crossing he
corners on

as if an old Cadillac
had died or two young were
marrying: other places

you see half-shamed,
sullenly-arrogant foreign
cars hugging into

clusters or, other
places, mixed bags
like university peoples'

GOD IS THE SENSE
THE WORLD MAKES WITHOUT GOD

Every year the hydrangea grows so
big its white brains, lobed nodes,
flop over all around the rim to

the first stormburst, leaving midbush
stem-arching open space: and then
the white booms, sprinkled weighty

by rain, turn green down near the ground,
splintery petal-balls: going high lofts
more substance than height assumes or holds.

PAINLESSNESS, TO PAIN, IS PARADISE

Does he know enough to know what it's like
to have been here: has he seen enough

to give seeing up: clouds, he's waited with white
October clouds like these often before

but when one white cloud shades another
gray, has he ever noticed that: and though he's

studied many falls' mottled casts, has he plucked
the wires of vines frost skins leaf-free: scrawny

notes! is more missing than was never enough:
he's certain certain loves absolve and heal in

passing rapids or welling stirs: but if he hasn't
done and seen enough to go, going itself may

pick up marks of rounding back to the beginning
where on the trek out who knows what perspectives

may improve or fall away and, last minute instruction,
a glassy light and, beyond, within that, dimly a brighter.

FLAWS IN DOMINANCE

Curious (or not at all) that now
we flash
language around the globe, our poets

retreat from speaking: they break
up and strew, smallen or blur oblique:
taking every brush pile, river

bend, scorched field into account
rives any sweeping account ragged,
peels any assertion into skinny

stripping: sects, tribes, pressure
and splinter groups assemble point,
partialities of definition, daring:

they know a place to get to and head
out: so is there any way or use
to address a level above all

or above number one and what notch
below the supreme receives any
message kindly right: rounded, we're

enwound: the engines of fragmentation
mean to cure themselves into
broad equivalences by destruction

and incorporation, whereas the languid
irresolution of world views (except
for negligible cells, pockets here

and there) breeds bumfuzzlement's
indirection: which are we more likely
to survive, the circumambient graces

of utter peace or the shiny-red
edges of anger and retribution: should
any voice rise to poise all hopes?

HOW THINGS GO WRONG

One person short-cuts across the lawn because
a new building is being added to the complex,
changing everything,

and his shoes press the grass over so
another walker sees a way already waged, and
pretty soon the root texture, like linen,

loosens on the ground, worn through: rain
puddles in a heelprint so walkers walk
around, broadening direction's swath: more

rain widens the mud so that given the picky waywardness
of walkers one could soon drive a chariot
right down the middle of recent developments.

ETERNITY'S TACITURNITY

It's so hard to tell what's missing: you can't
see by what is there: so little is there
that most of the time most everything is missing,

anyhow, intended or not: but all the missing is
easily missed because what is there, little as
it is, fills up the whole sight, blinding away

everything absent: and you can't tell what is
missing because absence leaves no trace: anyway,
I don't say anything about Rome or the architecture

of the Palatine: I say nothing about the Bavarian;
pre- or post-Christian; bureaucracies,
wars, canons, bloody murderers: in

fact, history which gives us the only identity we
have is so terrifying a tale I'd just as soon
wipe it out and keep trying to start over:

if I were to mention anyone, I'd mention old
Enkidu to whom I am unnaturally attracted; probably,
not Gilgamesh, he was so fretful: I almost never

say a word about where I came from: I left there:
please, when you see the little I have, try to
imagine what I've left out: I meant to leave it out.

KILLING STUFF OFF

These geese flying over now will be late
geese, the territories north already split

up and claimed: they'll have to fly
farther (north, north) till lichen's

the ground brush and chill never leaves the
nest: I wonder if geese do go that far,

lay eggs in frizzled moss and shrivel through
cold summers: geese mostly squabble over

at about the right time, error kept low by high
mortality among the very early and late: the

extremes are costly as usual, I'm afraid, even if
that's where persistency's invention cuts

most sharply new, necessity permafrost:
but there's no use to worry; things shape

themselves: still, in the short run, when
I hear geese going over this late, my heart
swerves, my throat jumps, late, late.

BOON

I put my head
down low
finally and said

where then do I
belong: your
belonging

is to belong nowhere:
what am I
to be:

your being is to be
about to be:
what am I to

do: show
what doing comes to:
thank

you
for this office,
this use.

DOWNSTREAM

It's a clear case with rivers: they
go on with the ongoing:
otherwise, darters headed upstream

would have no currency to keep true in:
parasites and speckled snails on
struck fronds or unshucked coconuts

wouldn't float to colonizations elsewhere:
riverweeds on wharf legs would flop sail-dull,
not dancing to point where the action went.

RUIN'S THE PALACE
OF COMMENCEMENT

Let the rousers through: I held on and
kept still; life, the unsettling possibility,
skittered by me: plow up the garden rows;
fury frolics: roll cornerstones, harrowing

hills: keep nothing recollection
sticks to: lust and vengeance start
fresh: shun libraries, retreats, the long
seminars of comprehending: greed already

understands perfectly: standing still this
way in the way of myself, I prevent what
I endorse, the letting out, the letting go,
the hour whose explosion fills to complete its time.

HOLDING HEIGHTS

Leaves evidentiary, branches
principles, trunk or stock
unity of source, the bush's shape's

elaboration's quick single, summary
like a feeling: underground, the radical
linkage provides ramification into

invisible foundation:
but the ground in all cases
prevails, taproot or desert-weed smokeroot.

The brook's slab-gray dry except
for flickers at a sloped slate's

narrows: all this gold, though a man just
down the street died young today:

I think to chasten the brook,
its diddle-flickers too brilliant

catching sundown, that it run smooth or
bend evenly for a change: but brooks

pay no mind: and, anyway,
maybe the flickering shells out a magic

that will spell this man over millenia
back to a perfect reconstitution in light.

MUSEUMS

The brook, running dry, will stop running, dry:
(it worms now like a lost rope down the slate roughs,
but it wrestles bank stones harshly after

downpours): slowed, it clears skinny dusk mirrors
with overhangs of branches that shade through
the stone bed into sky: the brook doesn't represent

beauty: it tears off a piece of shore moss, the soggy, threaded
bottom dangling in a strip: it sorts spill down ledges,
wears what it wears away, arcs in ice-like fangs or, skimming,

idles scum-floats: it doesn't fall apart representing
style: it means nothing but a sum of forces reacting
along a line to a sum of forces from whose sums the mind

makes up a day's subtractions, recollections. nothing
keeps it or wraps or hangs it up: but keep this
poem, this reminder not of keeping but of not keeping.

SECOND-RATE PERFECTION

Poorly-made people
burning accuracy alive
make the best verses:

those they make them
for are
away on missions words

play indifferent parts in:
the lame invent walking,
and the blind know

light's possibilities:
instinct seldom prowls
through to dumb

fulfillment: words are
briers to eat: in time,
the mouth no longer bleeds.

THE PLANET THAT WAS THERE

The snowflake knows
nothing, of course,

but for all it
knows, it could,

loosened from the blue
bottom of a cloud, drift

to the planet's
center,

except that willow withes
or tall brush or even

grass or bog-sphagnum
interrupt, and the so-long

journey that started
out

touches down, spending
its way at once,

flicks of momentum lying
about in mounds and lees.

TEREBENE SCENE

There being nothing left to tell,
one begins to speak up, curls and wisps
of interest, figurations, nest-like bits

and integrations set aside, for it's
not speaking the speakable, though
that can form grace or warp, but speaking

what can be said on the way to the
unspoken unspeakable — the place too deep
to plunder or else just a place cleared

off: the differences fall into
shimmering stations and stalls of gradation
back away from that well of difference,

indifference: from that well one drinks
the numb cold or lukewarm till not
cold or lukewarm, an intermediacy

appears whose balance wipes it out and then
nothing's there, and any fringe
incipience, floret, fury is

a grits-grain in starvation, the
marbling of lean in whiteside grease:
won't a theory be steered away from

its drive if bent in self-shade, forced
to serve formation not its own: but
what vine in fact gets through uncompromised,

curling — if one tries for the impossible,
no variant of the possible's left out, a prior
screening: people parties of one have

this philosophy, one person peripheral
could be the central one, oneself, so major
motions one ought to approve in the

population leave frail eddies of objection
around, not of the main flow, niggling
discomfitures, quailing critiques.

RAIN GAUGES

The fine branch twigs
are zipped noded

underneath with fine drops
and the big branch

twigs with big glassy
drops, but the finest

twigs nearly miss to catch
mist and drops

can't get big enough to
dangle from some limbs.

SAFE

I've hidden my desire over the wall under
a pile of stones the morning glory
never breaks out of (no white thread looking

that far through turned and darkened country)
and nothing ever comes in to:
so, possessed as the wind, I shake around a wider

country now, my paper-panther kite eyes
burning the leaves off trees with seeing and
rattling, brilliant, storming roots up into weeds:

stone held, I'm safe at last in vision.

READING TA'O CHIEN

Often I go out year-early
to the caterpillars' tents
hardly aweb enough in the branches
to notice,

and plunge a stick into
the core-squirm and,
twisting it, dip out a knapsack
bolus and chucking stick and

worms over the hedge say
well, little scribblers,
let's see you rewrite that:
this year, though, I'm — why I

don't know — so different, I pass
the cherry already an upright
lake cloudy with sail
and say to the late caterpillars

though they hardly listen
(at least, they don't reply)
what nice sentences!
the leaves sprout, the caterpillars

as tender as they, and both
purplish green: following the ravage,
for backup there'll be some new branches,
a second growth of leaves.

GEEZERLY

I stoop to slip a long
twig under the earthworm
drowning white in

the blacktop rainpool
so as to tote it
safe to the lawn's edge:

the worm loosens,
slack as the breathless
water but, nudged,

firms and lengthens
slender, needling for
soil: I can't

get down close enough
to work the twig under:
I'm too rickety to squat; too

brittle to stretch out
alongside: and
it's way too far to fall.

AN IMPROVISATION FOR
SOOT AND SUET

The pebble
fidgeted by freshets,
mouthed by
trout,
buried under bank shoals,
cleared risen by a falling tree's roots,
repossessed crinkled lacy by moss . . .

takes on the rondure
of attack from anywhere,

   its history its loss,
   surface events declared
   by vanishing,

   history what's
   left to tell what left

AN IMPROVISATION FOR THE KILLERS OF MEAT

The fat will let you weaken
before it will give in,
dissolve off into circulation
(resolution outmelts fat)
the liver comes between
to cushion,
absorb quick feed or
lingeringly to release held goods:
the guts dwell slowly
on a big feed
holding it back for the membranes
to nibbling polish away
or rush a small order through to
appease the responsive liver:
the fat resides
behind layers of
negotiation: you can't
flake it off, its
purpose to hold out and hold on,
bridging broad privations:

fat: first it is a sheet, then
a blanket, then pillow and bed
of pillows in which the empty stomach blinks

RECKLESS ENDANGERMENT

Black, red, gold, green-speckled leaves
mingle spotty on the same maple:

neighbors not seen all summer show
through the hedge: what

are they doing — raking leaves,
gliding sheets down billowless,

hefting airy armloads off to winded heaps:
what they're doing looks brighter

than the sweaty drudgery over here:
tools,

faces cleared this way
to view, though, someone could speak right

through the hedge, yard to yard,
and crack the summer's privacy wide open.

SWIMMING NIGHT

A train rumbles through the valley before day
and I think it at first a deep constancy storm wind
is rising and falling from but then the

whistle toots human signs and I try to pick out
roars, the wind's from the train's, but they
interchange or gusts tear up with a blanking

loudness I can feel the cedars tugging and whipping in.
Then trucktrailers whine like mosquitoes on the turnpike,
their brakes squealing at the light up by the airport.

ONTOLOGY PRECEDES TELEOLOGY

Appearances, undwellings, are shunted
aside, the come-and-gone debris

of the lasting, but, think of it, out
of the curvatures of time's plumbings, to

appear, be someone, in a where, a bit
planet in a furrow of a flimsy

galaxy, to show up
or show others up, endure being

shown up — just the flash
on the edge of time that cuts

things loose: to be present in the very
moment of emergence of what

is, spring moths or budsprouts or
peripheral novae or slur forms

ambling deep reaches: like that:
whereas we could love the lasting only

if it kept the present, which it
doesn't, but turns in and out of itself

until it turns free of weight
and shadow and becomes no more than

the turning in and out of its turning,
motion lost at last to a high undoing.

DISCLAIMER

A downpour, thunder-sudden and quit, rattled
then hummed the roof last night, but the woods,
so dry, soaked it up, the brook this

morning still a shimmer in silence: you can have
poetry in our time if there's no poetry in it, a
voice if it speaks without a voice: you can

have the world if you will have none of it and
honor if you can't see honor:
you can have wisdom if one

among the
clowns and looters, gigglers and angry castaways
will speak: flashy water travels

white over stone, the hard soft-worn,
but give up brook glitter and
the high world that shines immortal betides.

SPIKE-TOOTH HARROWS

We might, rather than lament nothingness,
make nothing of more things, ailments,
blunting the pain also of the differences
farthest from nothing, the tribulations,

shakedowns of self, forced competitions,
stagefrights we undergo without support
or wondering what the support
is, pills or terrestrial or

celestial friends: I long for a high
friend unfailing, for I have not met here
one who will not forsake —
whereas the celestial friend,

also, needn't be bedded down over the
weekend or awakened in a funk, or
lent money to, or encouraged himself,
but is constant, constant as nothingness

which we should not so much lament
as take to its wide ease,
a welcoming unsurroundable in expanse,
a quality of constancy beyond misfire; and

especially if there's nothing in us to betray,
no false structures, frail
arrogances to prop up, nothingness may
be, one to one, the very grail we quest.

PICKING WHERE OUT OF WHEN

Waiting's sometimes the most important element
in winning: for example,
suppose you decided to haul away

the pines' pollen cones:
you could get tuckered plucking, sifting,
break your knee slipping off risk-lengthened

ladders, stifle yourself with riled powder:
relax a couple of weeks, the cones clear off:
they may to an early thunderstorm even gold-fringe

puddles with dense flotillas and, afterwards,
dry into rings' finest meshings: so many things
left to themselves take care of themselves:

I know a man, though, who picked out his gravesite
and stone, priced the laying away, affixed
the stark period to his days, then

leaned back into every sine curve, swerve, coordinated
loop and swing of the grammar and loft of his sentence:
some things, a few, left to themselves,
needlessly prolong puzzling blurs.

ODYSSEUS FOR
EVA MARIA RODTWITT

Tying one to
one to
make one

and one to one
to make
another

and tying the
one to
the other

to make one,
soon
the design or

weave takes
the view
and takes

precedence till
the sharp flint
bit

untyable remains
that slits the
loops loose

so one can
tie one to one
to make one.

HIGH DESIRING

Though not the savior wished,
oblivion saves:

rememberers disperse, and
the grave, neutral as a moon,

rides in no difference
image or word can make:

united, indeed, at last — grave,
earth, father, child — there is

no further use, no scalded
eye, but the sweet of no

sweet at all, the perpetual song
words and music troubled a while.

THE DAMNED

This fellow grazed his woolly goats
on a high ledge, a very high place
snowless in summer, but it was,

perhaps because of the fellow's loneliness,
a region in which the mountains talked,
it seemed, and over a miles-wide gulf,

summits forever white rose useless
in august assumptions the polish of
the wind and glare of the sun sanctified,

the fellow supposed, and he thought,
well, few know that kind of thing,
a rare condition, though not good for grass:

and the fellow, noting that the peaks
had really said nothing yet, went to
the ledge-edge and looked down on the

summits of sweet-green hills
and runoff rills so lowly and supposed,
again, that these damned came of being

near the sanctified, wherever one finds
one one finds the other, and he wondered
if the heights knew, somehow, that the energy

of their complacency came of
a differentiation imposed on the backs,
so to speak, of the lowly, and he

wondered if the sanctified would not
wish to remove themselves, somehow, if
they knew that, but then, he supposed,

knowing that would spoil the sanctification
anyhow, so maybe the peaks could shine
there, since it seemed they had to, as

wastelands of what it means to be way high:
but the mountains had said nothing and
the fellow supposed himself a supposition,

too, no one having agreed with him, the peaks
too taken aback, except for this longing
for the valleys luxuriant in his depths.

WHAT WAS THAT AGAIN

If out in
the desert
we

trim the
billies will
the kidless

nannies die back
and absence
thin out

starvation,
and will
grass take hold

round ungrazed
dunes
and rise

closing off the
dunes like eyelids,
and will

brushwoods sprinkle
and flow into
the goatless hollows

streams can
arrive
shining in?

PRISONS THERE AND NOT

A feeling of transparency like freedom
accompanies choosing for oneself

what society chooses one to
choose: the ambience clears of brierworks,

and entanglements and the shades lofty
boughs catch from one another

become intangible with breeze: the DNA
puts its full intricacy behind one's doing

its calling, a boost uphill feeling
downhill: cleared spaces bigger

than fields open up around one and roads
run with one river-wide away

any way one turns: it's really
nice: fail to get off on the right

foot and have to turn aside for a cure
for having had to turn aside, though, one

causes, inadvertently, of course, delay
(ditches of delay running frittering systems

along those free ways) and misses dinner, picks
up a bug at the doctor's, finds, shortly,

one's desires nibbling away at accepted
practices: one wants to get free of

hindrances so one can get on with it, but
society isn't interested in hindrances, as

such: mixture, encouraging obscurity
of view, befalls, and one must devote

one's energy to re-addressing the clarifications
missed out on long ago: seeking to make way

through spent darkness, one construes a light
alternative to the light and begins to prefer its

small allowance as an opening, at least, or
something more like room than one had found before:

one's free choice then leads to a freedom not free,
but to a freedom free only following victory

over the freedom one originally fell out
with, meaning war: minority wars are hard

on individuals who even when they make right
minority choices live with their fellows

shadowed by a reality they're the exception
to: out of step, singled out, working as if as

usual in unusual frames, one cuts back
on preparation, aspiration, the dream of every

possibility: the branches of all this loss
heap up around one as a stricture: okay,

there is no help for this: one chooses to act
freely, openly: now and then one may

derive an instant's illusion of the freedom
missed, and tears may hollow out one's hollow cell.

MOVING FIGURES

Actuality surges,
swerves

into edges of
definition

or, vagrant, softens
and

parts or
stands

weightily awaiting
somewhere to

go (what is the
origin, anyway,

of let me put it to you
perfectly straight)

ALL'S ALL

A construed entity too
lessened to syllabify;
a mite or mote
dimpling
domy generalization;
a vague locus
(the flow of air

through prisons)
a puff of
the whiff of
a snail falling asleep;
stringy recollections of
fruitflies cruising
rosy bowlsful of

mangoes ripening mild:
ghostly leavings leaving
ghosts leave: retinal
worms empurpling
light scars
behind today's views:
bits of

retrenched nothings:
so much so,
little and all
alternately disappear:
the tiniest kiss
at the world's end
ends the world.

HARD AND FAST

A clarifying high
wind in October's
shanky last days —

maples luminous
mounds or
glacial hills dressed

down to shiny outline:
and thickets only
darkness traveled

through, clearly having
kept nothing worth
looking for: October

winds redress summer
tendencies, from
the litter of

freeze-scorched branches
to whistling gray
limb and clatter —

plenty of
clarification coming
ice can seal in tight.

SO LONG, DESCARTES

Once, trunks pitched into or
dragged down rivers, stones
cracked off or molded smooth

by exposure to edges, and living
trees, too, and all things
were spiritual, they flowed

with us in and out of seasons,
dispositions, everything not
without motion, and nothing was,

lived in our bones and went on
with our marrow at narrows' ends:
but then the ruler, the calculator

found and added up numbers,
groceries came to so much a week,
and sums and subtractions

slowed negotiations into form:
with access to little, we put
ourselves in charge of it: but, now,

our adding machines, as subtle
almost as the world, take in
quantities unimaginably specific

and broad, and now again we see
not established identities and
limits but the free flow returned,

the spiritual comings and goings
so dense, interpenetrant, and
responsive that tone and feeling

are our guide, and rivers, tides,
fronts, highs flow as they flowed
before, and we see with a trillion

events per second, hear and taste
in a flood, and live, if we live,
liveliest in this broad neighborliness.

MARGINALS

Some of these old widow women around here are roving
loners: no matter how deep the snow or bitterly near
zero the air, they're long-gaited out in their boots

of a morning and gone: one's high hip spins outward
every step, and one's eyes set ahead just above the
trees, and one hangs over a slouchy net bag lumpy at

the bottom, suggesting she could pack up and off
in any direction without regret, unsurprised: one
leans into a leaning shoulder, sidelong, as if eyeing

the ditch, as if listening with one ear (but
I've seen her on both sides of town in a morning): I
don't know where they go, probably not out to eat,

because they often don't have their teeth in: I don't
know what they do: mostly they just go, it's the motion,
going, I think, and, going, they rise through high

lattices till motion fills with song, their heads fill
with sky, and a wind rises in them like ecstasy or
death and, their minds made up, they let the earth go.

DAY GHOSTS

Spring thaw peels loose
the leaves snow caught
last fall before they
had really settled down:

now, a windy Sunday, they
stir over dry lawn
and remnant windrows of
ice, as if looking

for the place they'd meant
to go: but it's not now
as it was then
settling-down time, and

everywhere the leaves go
greens are
breaking out
amid the funeral arrangements

and the eyes of jonquils as if
hold on to their morning
tears and snowdrops, head down,
try not to look so bright.

NEXT TO NOTHING

Surely, choice in life isn't just a one-sided manufacture of mental boxes
to set out fluorescent along preferred directions nor mental blocks

to heighten retaining walls against rivers of self-insistence: surely,
there is interplay: just because a rein will sway the horse one way rather

than another doesn't mean you can get there without the horse, with just
a rein: surely, there is a shifting dynamics between artifice, as imposed

choice, and emergence, as that which finds its way: choice includes choosing
to be chosen by life, that is, choosing to be willing to be led out, like

a horse, into whatever options may perchance arise: but, naturally,
you don't want a horse just standing there steaming with incipience unable

to devote himself to rolling in the sand, say, or taking off at a gallop down
the freeway: you can't let a horse get up every morning and decide to do

something different: choice does not predominantly mean multiple choice, it
tends to mean narrowing imposition, settling for one thing and sticking to

it: adolescence is just a boiling off of puzzlings, polymorphous
possibilities, in order to cool down into a thing or two, mostly on top or

mostly on bottom with an occasional visit otherwise: let's say that after
adolescence you start to have sense, you start to make sense, and you start

making right on the top of the brain where the day to day mishmash of
decision-making chooses its ground, and then a kind of surface crystallization

forms, lattices drawing lines and leanings, that grown stable lets down
feelers underneath its structure searching for foundation or at least for

sodden mesh: so much of the mulch of brain is assimilated to or subsumed
by or overmatched by penetrant definition, so that after some years

you as much as have a wharf of piers along your negotiations; you may even
have a many-decked sealiner capable of setting out and returning relatively

unshaken: in some, fortunate or unfortunate, even the seas freeze, all the
ships tie up wherever they happen to be, the waves hold their steely

corrugations, the person lets life move around him, by him, an adequate
illusion of motion, and he comes and goes through the world with boulder-like

steadiness: such a person! how enviable in some ways, ways that the frail
and fluttery, the terrified starters and blunderers long to try: well,

every sweet thing drags a dull cousin along: would you want to storm an ocean
free just so you could take a little cruise: be choosy: live for others.

FOR MY BELOVED SON

The blackberries that ripened
soon after you left are

ripening again and thunderstorms
after the broken-down winter

are rolling through here again:
I keep looking for the season

that will bring you home:
I don't know how many times

I've put in the seed, watered
the plants, counted the blossoms.

OUTLINES OF ABSENCE

Teeth are distressing only
if you try to save them:
say there's a bit of rot

spotted under an old
crown, no way to get to it,
so the dentist recommends

splitting the tooth in half,
drilling out the dark, putting
a gold cap over

each root, then uniting the two
under a new crown: two little
shaved-thin roots sticking up

through the gum! the terror,
the dark journeys traced through
the night of maybe something coming undone

or not getting something right, the
whole invention maybe finally not
holding up, the little gold rod

stabilizing that molar to the rest
cracking or not quite
suiting its groove: the money!

whereas the poor and lost wait
unconcernedly, chewing away, till
the big tooth wobbles and they

yank it out: the relief! plenty
of bananas, whole wheat bread,
skim milk, the provender of paradise,

prove the bright flashes of
professionals mockeries and pinful wastes,
while the unsaved loosen wide smiles.

SAME OLD STORY

You turn to others
and leave
me standing there

with all the
responsibilities and none
of the rights

(and you never
wrong) but one
of these days

when you come
scratching back (backscratching)
looking for me, who

knows, I may be
dead and
gone or gone,

baby, I may be
dead and
gone or gone

BEAUTIFUL WOMAN

The spring
in

her step
has

turned to
fall

COGNOSCENTI

A little
money, you

know what
money can

buy; a
lot of

money, you
know what

money can't
buy.

CONTINUITY

I've pressed so
far away from
my desire that

if you asked
me what I
want I would,

accepting the harmonious
completion of the
drift, say annihilation,

probably.

GUNG HO

Arriving takes
destination

out
of destination:

the grave's
brink,

to late
years,

dismantles remnant
forwardness.

APPENDIX

Houdini died
not

of what
he

couldn't get
out

of but
couldn't

get out
of

him.

STAND-IN

A young woman
on the bridge tosses
rocks of
old snow

over the rail and leans to
watch them
streak
down into the gorge: all

the pleasures of
flight with
none of the harmful side
effects.

MAGIC

The wind across
the street blusters
a leaf over
snow till it

scampers up a

tree, flips
head down, fluffy
tail
straight up.

RARITIES

After thaws
and

showers, the
brook's muddy

(loud) but
as it

slows it
clears till in

summer
drought the

ledges clink
crystalline plinks.

OLD GEEZER

The quickest
way
to change

the
world is
to

like it
the
way it

is.

FINANCIAL SERVICES

Such a
greedy

man if
you

gave him
a

universe he'd
ask

for black
holes.

GROVE'S WAY

The campus oakgrove is
something (specially now

with the elms gone)
the branchlofts subsuming vast

congregations,
the trunks centuries through —

but a guy wire's been run
to hold in one

tree on the edge being
leaned out of the grove.

ROLLING REALITY

I saw a headless mummy out walking at dusk:
he carried his skull in the crook of
his left arm and with his right hand
made signs having to do with the reality
of consequence: sir, I said, you needn't

trouble yourself with dumbspeak for your
mere presence here startles knowledlge
of which saying's the puny part:
but the mummy held the skull into
my face, and it spoke perfect French,

I think, a tongue I do not perfectly
understand: but I said to the skull
(and to the mummy) if the dead aren't
dead (is that what you said?) then what
reality can clear this haunted coming?

THRESHER

I was made for another world, this
one, though, in stock:
so here I am: I hope you feel if not

great okay to stick around:
I talk, talk because like a mistake
on a grocery slip, if I'm not found

out, I lie unnoticed: what future dwells
in such a state: found out
causes a flurry, and passed over

boils and freezes reticence unbearably:
not for this world,
I twist and say so only to say so.

PUTTING ON AIRS

What oblivion is is total
reassimilation, not a
scrap of debris, stone-dust

blur, left behind, no
flinders of recalcitrance
cluttering the cycles,

ruffling the symmetry of the
wide-sweep rounding coming
round: who can bear the

hillside gully-washed to naked
flint, where so-and-so fell
down in prophecy's seizure:

or who wants to recall
Halicarnassus someone way
back came from: oblivion,

oblivion, residual of the
human common, how vacant and
bright, total and mutual

the gatherings there, the
blameless transparency,
the clear flow of desireless

desire, finding its way back,
back, back here to these suns,
stone-gripping startlements.

SUPERSTARS

When I find my new shape (hobbyhorse, roller
coaster, jet liner) I'm going to do plenty
and say so: I'm not going to bust around

fluffing and flubbing as if there were no items
to itemize, clumps to stack, deeds to deal:
I'm going to refer to and realize lofty images

(still playing them down) — such as the golf
tee of nothingness at the central spin
of mixing coordinations: profusion, profusion is

all and where possible (and even along with
lean necessities and little words) we ought to
have some, since not to have any may be

no more than the opposite choice: how
nervous to starve (and let others sink sunk-eyed)
on terms: when I find my new

shape (friendly, grist-hungry means) opulence
is going to perk out of jugs, hark in
hampers heaping high, and furnish stars additions.

STANDING ON THE CORNER
WATCHING ALL THE WHEELS GO BY

In a time of big cars, a small car raises eyebrows:
this law, lowly derived, is as high as any other sky:
contempt, amusement, curiosity: but if then the cars

switched, big to small, the law would remain the same:
another law, older than Kepler: (trilliums by the
trillion whitened the slopes broken down by brooks,

I noticed the other day as I rode in my car, small, as
it happened): I don't know: I just have a few words
to say: it's not my world, no: even though it is

the only world and, so, mine or not, mine, and I'd
better start taking the seriousness of it seriously
and taking responsibility for what becomes of it: well,

but what becomes of it can never be mine, never
approve my approvals, never affirm my root causes
and dreams but, quite beside the point, can poison and

parch my lacy innards, hard dry burnt ridges of good
stuff bleached weird, unearthly: so, not my earth, even,
which proceeds mainly by codes, pairings, nestings

I stand by and wonder at: too old a story to pity:
when the small car is the driving force of emotional
clustering, yea, when all the big cars are subsumed

in their similitude by the striking of a smallish difference,
more room's there for possibility than for pity: I
suppose this is doubletalk, vacuous wheezing on with

too little material substructure out of which under
other circumstance other sorts of flaring might
have flared: can one be lucky to be on the curb?

HOME PLACE

for G. P. E.

I'm walking with a friend
on his stony road
by Hatch Lake:
my son, six, is with us

and wants to race:
he knows we're old
and he could win: but what,
I think, if I have a heart

attack and hit
the ground: or
what if my friend does:
well, the sky's the same

here as anywhere: these are
universal trees: and stones,
nudged, roll down these banks:
okeydokey, I say: on your mark.

POSTMODERNIST VIEWS

I'm tired of looking at this old siding:
I've painted peeled patches winter
after winter till it's twelve shades of

white: when I walk around outside,
years light up in special collections,
flat flickers as from a churning mobile:

I'm going to call up and get a quick
estimate: I'm going to consider
color: I may try aluminum: or vinyl:

why not dye each side a different mauve
topped off with a prismatic roof:
maybe just hang with the patchy hues.

EXPROPRIATIONS

If you've
told somebody
once you
don't have
it still
to tell:
as the
mass of
your tellings
increases so
does the
scope of
your emptiness:
when perfectly
expressed you
are in
the plenitude
of speechlessness,
the wisdom
of not
a stir
to start,
not a
move's arc
to inscribe:
then the
bird sings
to your
whole world,
bone to
blue, singly.

NITTY GRITTY

If one can't be
somewhat impure
in his motives

(let principle
decay into circumstance,
wash multiple)

how can he
crack
light into

color, energizing
twinge, perspectival
warp, or

focus condensation
to a boil: the
slicing edge of

bitsy imperfection
gives colloidal
reflection to the flow,

point to
rise,
division to thorough bass.

ENFIELD FALLS

I don't understand why the stream
before the falls over by Enfield
reminds me of my own going through

things when it narrows to
a pass and sinks moiling through
a foot-wide sluice where the water's

so fast the banks back up: that
coming to a necessity, like being
born or dying or getting to the

dentist, that tensing and speeding
up, turbulence, and then the
opening out on the other side, easing

up, turning into sheets mist-thin
falling, air's weight, over
the fall's edge: I don't know

why this is and is not like things
I've felt: they say nature is almost
contemptuously beneath me now, I'm so

separate, my destiny so different
from water's, and I agree, at least, in
part, but also I don't understand why

what I have to take on, tense to, seems
easier, clearer, and more to be expected
just because water expresses motions

that look like my emotions: if
we could be a little at home here! . . .
racing, falling, easing away.

THE MANY WAYS NOT SUPREME

I didn't look for what I couldn't have borne to find,
I never looked, into a face where might be a face

I'd wholly wish, hands and fingertips, to
touch and trace, to hold in an instant eternal

forms an eternity of change could only affirm: no,
I might have seen and then what else might

my eyes have found to see: as it's been I've
watched faces flare, pass, flicker, or turn but nowhere

held still to that still face, adoration's feast:
the grave's lid can't close away the never known:

I'll take with me the blank eternity will leave from
then on blank, the unfound eye lively in my love's light.

SOJOURNING

I can see almost
as high as the Way
but not as high:

the Way too
high to see, though,
is only the high

Way: lesser ways
tangle at
times with time,

sway visibly —
foxgrape vines,
petunias — move

into recalcitrances,
boulders, but
up there

the radiance paints
no eager eye:
life's broken, low-down,

shadow-hardened, roar
and rot its
way through.

DEATH AND SILHOUETTES

Harassed with inquiry, I
waited up by a scale-flaked
boulder in a willow glen,

the pond there such glass
insects' dips riffled it
whole:

suppose the end gusts through
here someday, though,
I said. . . .

so let whatever is in being
meaning to be said out be said
unless this is where

saying gives meaning up,
the heart
airtight with perfection,

time come round at last:
glow
near dusk melted the pines,

the moonbridge's shadow
stone-stable
in water: may

the whole be touched
to push things on
after heart's-ease once? . . .

when a gull struck
the pond and lifted away
a minnow's whole absence.

FALL'S END

Glassy rain on the roads
and day melting down:

the bony hedges ink up,
tip-end inscriptions as if

scribbling out of here:
this prison is round,

the soul says, dusk
rounding into dusk:

the horizon's too gray
to part from the hills and,

now, the mist is too
fine to shiver

the puddles: remember broad
daylight: a redbird pitches

flickers in the shrubs,
a color beyond belief.

A PART FOR THE WHOLE

Feet burl up (knobs
knoll) peel, laminations

pleat and pleat against
wear, cushion

into calluses:
arches bone-sprung crack flat,

skin spins hard
(knit-whirls) into

thorns; the heelstring's
heelbone-hold

parches dry, itching
needles

to stitch pain's threads in:
what am I to do,

old feet: I
need you: wherever I've

ever been (jails) you've
walked me right out of there:

thick wide toenails
harden and slice

toe-meat: arthritis sucks

bone-mesh crunchy:

diabetic sores seeding
gangrene enflame

pus sacs: feet, good feet,
don't leave me up here with

the one place to go
and no way to keep from going.

LOFTY CALLING

Chimney-top, aerial- or cherry-tree-top,
Bob Shorter's mockingbird
splits daybreak to air-light glint glass,
chips slabs superfine, bubbles and pops

blisters, chisels light to pane-flint floats:
he wangles crescendos up from
cedar roots and sprays improvisations
into as many song-tips as cedar tips:

then with stark repetition
hacks a few cedars down:
he works at it — air's tilled over Bob's
place, tone-farmed: and then

at times, as if restless with stodgy air,
Shorter's mockingbird gets
the leaps and leaps on song swells
and settles down again as if into

buoys of his own music:
line and formation apprise the air;
invention on invention piled up
figure the invisible invisibly.

WEIGHTLESSNESS

Boulders high-lying
aside the woods'
ridge compress

light: if the light
sprang out of them
they would be husks,

foggy crusts: where
dreams rise
to the hemlocks have

resettled, within each
green a golden
form: nature

comes back from
transcendences, rounding
out the motions'

necessary rondures:
here in stump-meal
the worm parades.

ROSY TRANSIENTS

A wretchedness will come with an improvement, like as not,
just as, on some occasions, a bright morning will be
bitter windy, the weeklong cover having at least held warmth in:

the balances of mix's interpenetrations are subtle enough
to add up to or derive from consistent gray but because the gray shades
off into hues and because some hues statistically bend banding together

away at intervals reinforcing one another, some days are brighter
than others and as relief from dark oncomings bright dwellings
more or less reside: but this variety! — your

biggest winnings could become too much wealth to care for
(and nothing else to do), as your greatest happiness
could drag you to surgery and a big-eyed abortion: and

anxiety, on the other hand, that strings your striations up and flails
them dry, can reorder your priorities: getting away
with something — no, the strictures and self-strictures are thicker

than the liberties, but with a pittance you can get away, the price
tag attached, no discount applying, and no hidden weapon: all
men are equal, or nearly so, in these just systems dull as dust.

THE INCOMPLETE LIFE

At the extreme
tip of
the future is

death, of course,
and short
of that something not

much like life,
a careless caring
and pain perhaps

one's
ceasing ceases: an
experience whose

experience shuts
experience down:
at the

moment one has
the whole world's way to
say one

is beyond words,
just words,
just beyond words.

CHOSEN ROADS

A snatch of crabgrass broken through a crack in the blacktop,
suddenly a watery-bright earthworm flips out whole into the
midafternoon sun and hitting the scorched macadam dances

in loops across six blistering inches to the margin's shade
and ground, when another follows flashing into the light but
strikes out at a longer angle for the edge and stretches one

end to the shade, not before the other sticks to the starved
heat and dies: the safe end wrestles tugging this way and
that to get loose but the burnt end, hard dry, holds.

SUMMER PLACE

The ocean will grind, yea or nay, the sky gape,
spiders will shake their lines, and cuneiform will
become photooffset or something or nothing: when

you consider the wreckage expectation and delivery
will wreak on each of us, though, it's a good thing,
probably, that other things and people won't care

about us as much as we do, thus moderating our own
cataclysmic perspectives: when I go, I shake the
universe I know loose: that this shakes me

more than the universe is some comfort, about all
I'm likely to get: everything that isn't trivial
could be made so: that would help keep things down:

my last fallacy of imitative form, my book on
roundness, disappointed me some (oh, yes, it did), I meant
to write one unreadable, but a lot of people have

bought it, reading it or not: I wanted something
standing recalcitrant in its own nasty massiveness,
bowing to no one, nonpatronizing and ungrateful:

I don't know why: maybe I'm just tired of the world's
inroads, the small invasions where my little landscapes
are stripped, defoliated, re-arranged:

or tired of being put upon by this and that person's
demand and need and having to swelter inside
with the moral melting of whether to do this and that

or not: this morning, I got a letter from this
Arkansas lady who runs a bookstore she says isn't
doing too well, and she wants me to sign a stack of

bookplates to help my books move: I already last
year signed a bunch of my poems she had typed up on
separate cards: I haven't forgotten I did that and

here she is back again: am I being played for a sucker:
if I'm being played for a sucker, which is the thing
to do, blink and be generous and help her even if she's

prevailing upon me or set the stage that I'm on
to her and throw everything in the trash: it's
not doing the thing, it's being put on the spot and

having (being made) to make a choice: that energy
of decision is costly: you can't just make one
decision and follow through, every decision is

different: it isn't easy, what would you do: then
there are the recommendations, ooh, la, la, the letters
of recommendation! no postage, no envelopes, no forms

filled out — just the command, send a letter of
recommendation to so and so: or send a dozen: still
no stamps, no envelopes, no forms filled out: you

get the picture: so thinking of an imagined land, I
thought of a big gritty poem that would just stand
there and spit, accommodating itself to nothing and

too disfigured to be approached, no one
able to imagine what line to take: and not necessarily
being interesting enough to invite anybody to read it:

nothing turns people off like complaining, they get
enough of it doing their own, so why not have a
complaining poem: that could core your reality and

stack up the peelings: Gary and I just went over
to check out Corsons Inlet: there were a lot of bugs:
(fellow said they said on the radio Fargo, North

Dakota [I thought that was in Nebraska] had a foot
of rain and the Red River, can you imagine, flooded):
this is not going to be another one of those free

association poems: this one is going to be all about
complaining, so there's no point in getting limbered
up for heavy swerves, this is going to run right down

the centrality, clickety-clack: at Corsons Inlet they
had the Least, Arctic, and Common Tern, but the Least
were raising the most babies and the most hell: they

made a community project of hovering, circling around,
diving, and screeching: but we found the young about
hiding in the stalks of compass grass and right out

on the clam-shell white sand were indentations,
nests, one or two eggs in each: we walked
crisply on the clam shells so as not to step on the

eggs: then we stopped at a place for a dollar's worth
of ice tea, two fifty-cent sizes: it sure was hot out
there on the sea plains but the ocean has added another

seventy-five yards to the headland: (the same land it's
been subtracting from the north end of the island where
bulwarks and jettys are doing very little

to retain the retaining walls:) how does the ocean
get into these persistent notions: it's hard not to get
interested in something: there seemed sheer strength

in the numbers of blackflies waving over and sucking on
the inlet strand, multitudes, you kick them up before
you like sand or, more persistingly, like fog: you know

they all have to be doing the same thing approximately
because there're too many of them to be doing different
things: just like the sand-ripples on the headland, how

could you design something that all looks alike but every
one is different: a studious drawingboard: same with
the lacework castings of the sandworms, a filigree

incalculable, though pretty much the same: so it's all
there, who wants to be stunned by it over and over:
desire is incredible anywhere and I have a lot myself:

insatiable because unsatisfied: yep: burning all the
time doing time in the dungeon: if it got loose it would fire
off an acre of trees: this is my worst complaint, that

desire often has to be held back and stanched: but
holding back gives you plenty of energy to complain with:
look for a long piece: a windstorm just struck up

a sandstorm here, the winds going quite precisely from
easy-going to whistling, a sharp change, hard enough
to walk off with a tin shack: and the storm so

fast, it seems to have no lightning in it — and
no rain, a blower, mixing too many levels perhaps
for charges to build up: but somewhere back there in

the west is a nucleus, storm center or cell,
for all this commotion: I hope there will be some rain
to lay the dust: but how nice to be cooled off: ninety

degree days are not as nice as less than ninety degree
days: nice to see trash rise, swirl, slam against
houses and linepoles: beach chairs bloom woven

bottoms and kilter off like the awkwardest bird
across the beach: sand in flumes spills like water
down into the surf, frying in a frying: I'm in this

place and everybody is having this banquet, except me,
I have this dry crust I'm nibbling on: so I say, how
come I'm not having a banquet like the rest of you guys, don't

I have as much right as anybody: the banqueters say,
hunger will sharpen your perceptions and your perceptions
will be useful to us should we ever get hungry:

oh, flubbery flubs, I say, neologizing: I don't care a hang
about your perceptions or mine either, I'm hungry: if
I can't have any of what you're having, give me

something else: you would be surprised at the fat indifference
of people at a time like that: call them a bunch of
hogs and go off and eat the wind, what else: and suckle

the rain and pretty soon you're a nature poet, everybody
saying, lands, something nice to go with dinner, they say he
enjoys plants and feeds ants, a luminous starvation:

I have this theory about when people want you to assume
the position of maximum receptivity or penitence they
don't tell you to sit down but to get down on your knees:

that, in relation to the person who just told you to
get down on your knees, leaves you looking into the
genital area, a dark, winding, if absorbing, subject:

in that position you can receive the rod of knowledge
head-on, or if you don't receive it, you can get the
image what you could receive if you don't do right:

almost anybody would rather do right, specially if the
commander is a beast: where this puts some men and women, who
might get a small thrill from the warning and who might

not decide to do right, I don't quite know if I haven't
already said it: but it appears that the sexes *are*
different, if equal: hustler or hooker, different

postures suggest different approaches: any way to make a
buck, if you consider that one amoeba eats
indigestible sand which it pushes out to the periphery

of its protoplasm to form a casing, a little house
not all flesh: a nature poet would be the first to
tell you that any way to get by is worth exploring:

of course, I don't mean to say anything mean about
ants or other clever insects, builders, twirlers,
weavers, stickers, and domicile developers: ever

since, which was some time ago in reading Wheeler,
I heard about the ant that attaches itself to the
chamber wall and allows itself to be fed till it's a

honey storage tank, well, I've been touched: it
reminds me of myself in reverse. I've been storing
up honey in civilization but though much emptied out,

I don't get any emptier than I've always been: I was
born on a farm and had to work and never got much
book learning or much interest in it but I don't mind it in

others, really, provided it doesn't swell to cause
nonconversational flotation: I object to much bobbing
while I'm talking: I prefer people who simmer down

and change the subject often, without flightiness: I
don't like people who flit from branch to branch of
the learning tree so fast I can't spot their majors

from their minors: but then I don't like people who
take off to say something and then just quit midway:
it's like leaving a bird permanently between bushes:

I can tell you right now I don't know how to write
verse, not even poetry: if I did I wouldn't be here,
so to speak: I'd be off on a Greek island with Merrill

or in the radiantly inaccessible regions with Ashbery
or vanishing into the clearest plenitudes with Merwin
or reading from my works to the Poetry Society of

America or South Orangeburg or I'd be mumbling among
the members of the Academy of This or That instead of
just sweating it out as America's Least Likely Issue:

that is, don't send me your poems, please, for comment
and/or criticism: I don't know what to say: not only
don't I know what you should write, or how, I don't

know what or how I should write: if I did I: I'll
tell you what I do do, though: if I think of something
I give it a whirl: if it comes off, well, it's

merciful: if it doesn't, I still can't throw it away,
but I keep it around hoping it will flare out or up eventually:
join or form and join a local group where you can share

your poems, see what others are doing: every now
and then read a good poem, if you can find one you didn't write
yourself: I'm interested in you: but I can't, since

there's one of me and fourteen billion of you, answer
all the letters and provide hopeful hints: I say
there's only one of me because though every letter

begins "I know you must hear from a lot of people but"
what every letter means is forget about those other
people and give me your undaunted attention: this that

I'm complaining about is not metaphysical: don't look
to hear from me: I don't have the secretary, the
postage, or the know-how to come back at you: believe

me: why is it that doctors expect to be paid for their
time and lawyers and bowling coaches for their
time but nobody expects to pay a poet: I guess poets

are supposed to be so used to poverty they don't need
any money: I suggest you send your poems to Galway
Kinnell who knows a lot about the art of poetry or to

Richard Howard who can afford the postage: don't send
to John Hollander who knows so much about the art of
poetry you wouldn't understand a thing he said:

what gets you around here are the raunchy, skinny
bellies of coeds with the pear-like rump rondure
sloping the dinky-little bicycle seats: wouldn't

it be fun to be leather: such starvation, what
gauntness of sinew and vein, what personal hairpullings
and twistings with the sheets, what hold-overs and

backorders, what lineations described with delight's
elaboration, what fingers in.the mind twiddling, flicking,
what sudden bombastic progressions and reversals, what

braidings and upbraidings of the rope of the self, what
profiles, weights, curvings inward and outward, what a
time I'm going to have with women's movements, Adrienne

is going to give me the sullen, if understanding and
patient, eye and then burst into an oratorio of
verse-like abuse! Denise is off there by herself, now:

she won, her victory our embarrassment: how I wish I
would hear from *her*! what old-style men wanted of women
was to get them down, fill them up, and go play golf,

leaving the ladies to simmer in fruitfulness, wondering
what hit them, drenching and draining: new-style men
have to remember that ladies like to play golf, too:

a quaint plainness with full-scale cool reservation and
qualification qualifying qualification, rhythm undecided,
and explosive small gesturing: somewhere in there is

the truly heroic scale, the mind at a sufficient standstill,
the underview amounting to a wide cancellation like
space: oh, if only one could get to it, without

meanwhile raising a bristle! how delightful to be so
accomplished you're completely unread! practically too
much to imagine with coolness: well, it's the 4th or

firth of forth and last night's storm cleared the air
which, however, filled the highways this morning, every
other Philadelphian coming down to regard the waves

and the other Philadelphians: what a herculean act of the
imagination to imagine Philadelphia imagining itself in America!
you could draw a sharp line around Philadelphia, take it out,

and no one, not even non-Philadelphian, would notice:
I guess it's because so much of our heritage is buried
there: a prayer for flatness: what do

you do with flatness: you can't pray for it, prayer
too much into high rise: you could say, today I'm to be
flattened out on the floor of the self's sills:

sublime (or counter sublime) as I am, I walk back from
the beach by all the bathing beauties and bathing boys,
and by the older folks in good houses, and I feel like

a bit of country trash, a splint of nothing washed up on
the planks of time, and I feel impressed that all those
people have made something important of themselves with

less cloth, probably, than I have: I hand it to them
(the importance, but I would also hand them the cloth)
and think, how nice for you, you've found a suitable,

dense smallness of the exact gravity and grist of your
body, and there you are, unfloatingly answering the
universe, that is, being integral with it and paying it

no mind: I found a dime on the way back: that's the
interest on two dollars for a whole year or maybe the
interest on a million dollars for a second: the faucets

here have water misty with microwaterbubbles, milky
in look: I fill a glass and, though trash, go ga-ga,
marveling, something I do circumspectedly and limitedly

these days: the bottom starts to clear as the bubbles
rise and pretty soon you start to hear a fizz, specks
of peppery water flying off the surface: and when the

fizz is wildest, a motion counterclockwise commences,
as if the motion in the airiness could take hold or
express itself better: then I observe that the bubbles

don't break in a continuous fizz but rapidly flash in
patches big as your index fingerprint: when nearly all
the bubbles are gone, the motion ends and fringe reefs,

as around atolls, stand like a long foam: I figure with
precise instruments, I could discover a lot, quite
useless, probably: the marvelous useless, though, seems

more marvelous than the useful marvelous: but I just
drink the water: soothing occlusion: where can I find
any junk: every street or alley I look into bedazzles

me with poetry, the call to naming, to saying forth,
to being said forth: when I get the fences, lightpoles,
ladders, plastic tricycles, cracked concrete slabs all

together in a heap the heap will round up and bloom
into the shapeliest rose: today, I am filled with anger,
the worst-looking thing in the house or on the street:

it's a fifth: last night they had a fourth, a boom-boom
show, pow, pow, k-choom: everybody that could get
there got there, wheelchairs, forearm walking braces,

canes, four-footed canes, tricycles, bicycles, motor
bikes and cycles, skating boards, and jams and jams
of cars: one ought to try to define what is so great

about a fireworks (firewords) show and then design a theory
of poetry around the definitions: I guess colorful
explosions are, by all odds, what we most adore:

and then, even more, colorful explosions that assume
sky-high figure, umbrellas of downspinning, metronomic
regularity of hard staccato with the punctuating white

terminal stab: dit, dit, dit, dit, WHAM: and the
transitoriness of it all, worse than day lilies, calls
out the hunger of immediate appreciation or loss of

life: everybody wants a community of shared perceptions
and with fireworks you get the community: last year
we had a well-publicized poetry show and attracted

fifteen people: half of them, approximately, were the
performers, and the other half, scattered and roped
wives, husbands, cousins, intimate friends: it was

not a good show: if you want the community to turn out
don't build a church, ballet theatre, sound stage,
art museum or any of those expensive, cultural things:

this is the difference in a democracy: the money is
where the people is: in the old days, the money was
where the people wasn't: so, I guess we'll have to

adjust: 199 years independent, we may learn yet that
a servitude to numbers is still servitude: and worse,
the few are run out of face into comedy at their

gatherings, having no glitter of diamond, even, to sanction
the glitter of mind: our artists to the trash pile!
of course: well, let us make a mess of trash:

politically equal (in theory), let us begin to form an
aristocracy of life (in fact): (let us make certain
our group does not form out of public, governmental

funds: wherever there are funds, mediocre managers
gather to swivel and sway: they create objectives and
the objectives are wrong: they create evaluations and

don't know what they're talking about: they seize the
power stick and they know they have the right instrument
and they "help" you right out of your mind: ta ta:)

this is Feeding the Fucking Sparrows Day: why not:
they make a round table out of a slice of bread:
an occasional fluttering, peckery disagreement, but

then right back to it: funny, though, they eat the
table which, nonArthurian, goes from square to round, then
tears away in chunks till it's flown away as all-day

providers: over nothing there is no disagreement: but
it's hard to keep Feeding the Fucking Sparrows Day from
becoming also Feeding the Fucking Starlings Day and

Feeding the Fucking Grackles Day: purity needs a
mixture to know itself by: a lively play of the mind
over the particulars like wind over the inlet tide:

tomorrow we will have another Day called Listening
for the Sparrows to Cut the Fucking Cheese Day: yesterday
was Independence Day: someday we will have to call a

Day Interdependence Day. neither sincere nor serious,
I hesitate to engage anything above the level of a
broken bottle for fear of being, in a free state,

misunderstood or investigated: questioned closely, I
would have to admit that the America I love is hardly
in prevalent view so it must be somewhere hiding around

weeds, fencerows, windowboxes, railsidings, and abandoned
roads: hiding around abandoned roads is a good one:
what would you say differentiates the highminded from

the lowdown good-for-nothings: clearly, it's a matter
of altitude: but altitude in terms of what:
perhaps, it is representativeness, including the

principles of synopsis, assimilation, concept: then
there's high society as over and against the low, common,
and vulgar: then there are high places (where the rich

live): everything high appears to be desirable except
high meat prices: why is that: I'm just sure that our
fundamental image is hierarchical, disposed like a

mountain with the wide and numerous low shrinking to the
narrow and lofty few: thank goodness, I'm the very
peakstone of something, a mt, though I don't know how high

it is: it is not as high as General Motors or even
Anaconda Copper or Kennecott: it's about as high as
up to here: anyhow, I'm sitting on it: it feels good:

bowling champions make twelve times as much as poetry
champions: pool sharks about ten: tennis, fifty, etc.:
poetry is a range of ridges which, however, rises:

since (life is a terminal disorder) to choose to gogo
forward into life, or a makeshift thereof, is also
to choose death, it's hard to get everybody up and out in

the morning bushy with appetite: but nature to
prevent bitching makes it bindingly easy on us by
providing only one way to go(go), choose it or not, a

half-reassuring nudge or fate-motif that relieves us
of the responsibility for any ultimate disposition
to things: the sparrow lights in the steel fence mesh

and cheeps: (note the two orders of statement: one
is endlessly expandable and conditional and the other
firm and complete): we had the fifth last night: I

mean that last of the fifth: today is the sixth: last
night was the drum and bugle corps competition: every
corps should have won, although some should have won

more than others: I liked St. Ignatius from Hicksville
best though, although the leader was great, I liked the
leader of the first corps better — the Black Watch, I

think: she was heartbreakingly beautiful: I loved her
instantly as I must love her forever: though she was
in perfect command, she was not commanding: that is,

command was not so much in question as to be required:
her high-stepping stills were all the same,
rigorous and to the exact height: when she walked,

when she walked her right fist came to her chin, her
left hand flicked out behind her, completely feminine
in a total dignity: she never once seemed self-conscious

or out of role: even in her salute to the audience
her participation was altogether with the corps: at
the end, when the corps paraded by the stands, she did

not yield a flicker of acknowledgment but held her part
strict and clear: the other leaders, grand as they
were, introduced some spoiling bit of sentimentality or

grossness: ah, when the thing is flawlessly done! and
done pleasingly, not to please: it is an unbearably, I say,
noble and generous use of the self, a beauty beyond

every demand or contingency, a beauty in itself: this
is not a matter of content or invention: the creator
of the routine has his own place: this is performance

when performance itself creates clutches of value: I've
heard performers, musicians, dancers knocked because
they were the puppets of original genius but performance

exceeds creativity into its own genius: this is the beauty
of "Do the villanelle and shut up": here I'm
working the antipode, the exact opposite: the slouch,

the shambles, the crying out, the sore toe, bum knee
after the show is over: but this is the sixth: it
is Feeding the Fucking Sparrows Again Day: it's the

same if you look for junky language: in a way one hunk
of idiom floats swirls of energy as well as another:
get your afflatus flattened, it just takes on prevalence:

masturbation is handy, cheap, and clean: it engorges
itself on phantasy, the line between the imagination
and the seminal vesicle direct: hit the right image

and you come immediately: the scrotum is the conjurer's
bag of stones, bones, trinkets that are spilled out
and sorted through till the sought image turns up,

inflaming in its finding, desire seized and placed
in context and given course: these little trinkets
touch off the deepest reservoirs of the self, unlock

releases, the truest version: deepest are images of
the other, or the same, or some detail or part of the
other or the same, or even an image of the whole

spiritual self of the other, or an image of the other's
response, as seen in eyes or felt as through the central
line of the imagination: any way to get there is the

necessary way: any way that leads away ranges farthest
and most accurately when it keeps its holding there:
so we are in ourselves men and women, some of us with

phantasies that derive from and play into reality, some
of us with phantasies reality cannot support or fulfill:
nevertheless, crippled or distraught, we are members one

of another, truly, and must appeal outwardly to rights
and responsibilities: it is hard to be whole, unless it
is quite easy: anyway, we know, as when we hug a son,

the spirit *flows*, it moves from the full self into the
need: the transportation feels actual and
physical: similar transmissions occur when one's arms

are around the beloved or when one thinks of a friend
away: these are the knowledges that lie lowest and rise
highest in us: the bailiwick of love that best allows

and describes us: still, it is so hard to write
significantly of insignificant nothingnesses: until
the poet comes, Wilbur or Wakoski, we must wait to see:

yesterday was 7-5-75: today next year will be 7-6-76:
then there will be the once-in-a-decade 7-7-77, century:
boy, innertube, and creek: get away with this: you can't

go by me: cutting figures gets a big hohum: why's a man
like you a man like you: rock has gutlevel appeal,
simplicity, and story line: plowed fields patched here

and there with brilliant standing water: Yeats would
have been okay if he hadn't named his wife George:
careful that the truth that sets you free doesn't kill

somebody else: the poet of nature or of civilization
reports a human seeing: the longest thing in North
Carolina is Sunday morning: sex is at the bottom of

things: circle around the truth without telling
it and you tell it: clearing, thicket: a poem
is a thicket whose clearing is disposition: you find

as much interest in the world as you have in it: you're
practically rotten before you're ripe: day makes light
of night: (realism, mimetic representation: copying,

in different dimensions and modes the apparently real
world the way it, to all appearances, really is): there
are two heavens, one is this world's pleasure: the other

is release from this world's pain: well, the juice has
expired and the therapy has run out of this: it is the
next day, no apparent improvement over the preceding:

it is Monday, July 7, 1975: the big weekend is over,
including, I hope, the all-night bouts and brawls in
the house next door where a bunch of young fellows are

doing a little renting: the music loud and bumpy from
midnight on, the girls in gales of hightalk and humor,
the men resorting to blows: the motorcycles at 3 a.m.

tearing up the backyard and getting stuck in the beach
sand of the tearing: a kind of middle class, vacationing
howl: I should call this Get the Fuck Out Day: but to

where: *this* is my last resort: the dog across the street
that for two summers hung over the fence yelping to
whistling hysteria at every passerby till two in the

morning has been stationed back a ways behind the filling
station: he still yaps but not with such proximal
intensity: to make up for it, the lady next door has

acquired a youngling which barks with youthful expectation
whenever possible: the noise level here is the sound
equivalent of the trash level, including trashtruck noise:

poets have no intention of saying what they mean: so
they say something else that means what they mean:
this reeling looking-around connects disparate areas

and through gravity compels them to form a globe;
similitude and metaphor having arisen: in swerving
away from the direct telling, the poet incorporates

related areas of the world within his swerves, the
bindings of avoidance: I spend a good deal of the
day rocking on the front porch girl watching: or

boy watching: what with the long hair and slender
shapely backs you can get pretty far into admiration
before you realize it's a boy: that's a puzzling,

stalling, acrid feeling, going in under the concept
girl and backing out under the concept boy: well,
we're told to love everybody and such confusion makes

it a lot easier: I wish everybody would go to his
library or neighbor and find out what ragweed is: then
if everybody would just see to his own place, we could,

I'll bet, get all or most of the ragweed pulled up today:
it's not that hard to pull it up, specially the month
before it blooms when it stands about a foot or less:

I just pulled up two plants growing at the foot of the
telephone pole next to the gas station: then I pulled
up in five minutes a sight of small plants behind

the gas station where there's a discontinuity of soil between
the street and the elevated pouring for the station:
if everybody on his lot would get together and pull

together, we could plink every plant out in an hour:
of course, ragweed pollen is so fine it will float in
from anywhere: but local effects can have some effect:

let's try it, everybody: pitch in and pull up: some
kid or assless old man or watery-thighed old woman might
get a little relief: relief is what we're after: I've

been so overstimulated lately it's been frantic: I've
screwed and otherwise engineered myself down to blanks
but the continual flow of barefooted, half-naked nymphs

by the door, and firm, phallic-bodied youths, has
kept me in a constant, surprised knowledge of the reality:
I really don't know what else to try, to get relief from

relief: I'm afraid I'm going to wear myself out: back,
as far as I'm concerned, to Feeding the Fucking Superego:
or Counting the Cottonpicking Cracks in the Sidewalk:

this one gal last night at the gala said, "That's not what
my father said, my father said, 'If you get pregnant, I'll
kill you' ": and this morning as I was pricking along the

sidewalk, I heard this lady on the second floor porch say,
I'll be glad when I'm a senior citizen, the senior
citizens cash in on so many advantages, I can't wait till

I'm a senior citizen: said she: now, that, I thought, is
the way to do it: I was pricking along to the library to
look up *trash* in the unabridged: I got it all down,

every bit of it, including the *white*: even the bottom
leaves on tobacco, cropped first, sandlugs, when cured
brown and papery: I bought my first bicycle when I was

15, I think, by being given the first pickings of the trash:
I'm not just trash or white trash or country trash, I'm
tobacco country trash, high-principled Scotch-Irish,

poor white, redneck, riffraff trash: I know all about
it: and a lot about the other trash around: I take a
trashy view of things: but, then, baby, I love what

I know, and I know trash, there's so much of it, democratic,
everything turns into it, and so few people want
it, there's a surplus of it, pick up free: now, when Stevens

got on to the prospect of a coat-of-arms or royal lineage
back there in Dutchland, he plowed a little money into
discovery: my money's in the bank and here and

there, and, right now, thank you, I don't need any: the
only royalty I'm ever going to be interested in is royalties:
more and more, there're going to be so many I'll

sway back and dig imperialism: from where I started the
route was up or forget it, and I've come most of the way:
people have heard of me never heard of Amenhotep, who swayed:

I'm a born aristocrat, as anybody will tell you: it's
unfortunate there were no funds to carry me off: I
recognized the poet, the trashiest breed, right away as

my most perfect and friendly apprehension: so I have
become if not king of the cats, prince of the hogs & snakes:
it tightens my nose and makes me feel possum-hungry just

to think of it: I'm going to sway my trash around until
every elegance wilts: nobody has established a more
cordial relationship with the heights than I have, a fact

which has already caused the elegance to shrink even before
it's going to have a chance to wilt: but my sway will, as
time goes on, become the new elegance, bumpy and roughshod:

take the old geezers and other rest-home spindly drifts of
flesh: now, that's *trash*: or how about all
the mentally retarded or disturbed children or old folks:

lesbians and queers of all varieties: migrant workers,
not getting anywhere: strung-out guitar pickers at
hopeless junction so and so: aging hookers and johns who

helped with the tide: retired persons: little old
ladies floated up in Florida, no husband, no home,
no children who want them, and not enough to eat:

we should call this The Republic of Barrels of Trash: we could
now be entering the bicentennial year of The United States of
Barreling Trash: "pretty soon the people on welfare gone

be richer than working people": The United States of
Shining Garbage from Sea to Greasy Sea: the litter
glitter: all that remains of free enterprise is if

you fail you deserve it: the land of the hopeless case:
the land of the biggest lobby: we know what is right:
when are we going to make it right: every legislature

knows but what's right is so plain it's embarrassing:
the corporation, the military, the agency: the power
blocs: all have exceeded the guidance and correction

of the people: can here and there an honest man stand
up and not lose his job: can here and there a
decision-maker decide what he knows he should: not

very likely: it's okay if some have more if others
have enough: well, get out money for the trash to meet
my pure country trash platitudes: I have not given the

matter under study much study: I'm going to study up on it:
surely, lean, firm energies and rightnesses are found unanticipated
in free competition: but then you need to be sure the

competition is not rigged: surely people who find
and make things deserve to be rewarded: but the lean,
firm energies throw some people aside: we need to keep

the energies but we need to correct them from abuse,
the particular cases of mischance, sharpfallen destitution,
of suffering and disaffiliation: we need to sustain the

fallen and extend opportunity to the fallen who can
rise: it is not a great country that grinds along on
the spills and breakage of the weak: it may be strong

but it is not noble: this is a noble nation: it must
be great and noble: it must do what is right to do:
it must hold back the chomping greedy, nourish the needy:

my trouble as a propagandist is that I want everybody to
be right (and, of course, happy): but is that, like,
nobody right or happy: ah, these spheral men: they

stand there looking all ways till their feet rot off:
what we need is for someone to choose one thing instead
of another: and choose something that will carry at

least a 60/40 ratio of good: when in again pops the spheral
man in a wheelchair saying, well, then, get it on
up to 90/10 or 100/0: and there you are: if we could

make a kebab of principle and skewer our chunks of
expedient deals with rightness running through,
the republic might shine otherwise and we could

call it The Land of Rightness Shining Through the Roasted
Morsels: everybody knows it's the awkwardest
thing each one standing around the fire with a raw piece

of meat in his hand, shoving and snitching and
forming Cartels of Power to the Flames, or Clearing
Little Guys out of the Way to the Fire: a few

principles could lend so much structure to deals there'd
be a lot less haggling over shady adjustments of the
moral or morsel self: but who will rise and announce

the structure of the elevations: who will accept the
skewer of backbone in his own hanging meat: if the
government becomes unworthy of the people, it's a fine

opportunity for someone as worthy as the people to get
up and say, the people are worthy, and I am worthy:
the machine probably wouldn't re-elect him but what a

button of fresh air, could get to be habit forming: I
went over to the Atlantic this morning and said, simply,
long may you wave: the Atlantic didn't say anything

but it waved: put yourself in certain places, it will
be thought of you automatically that you don't amount
to anything or you wouldn't be there: au contraire,

get, by hook or crook, in to other places you will
automatically be thought something: there is, then,
obviously a genius to a place, a place spirit; for

example, the bar of the Fontainebleau has not quite the
aura of a coffeehouse: likewise the executive suite
at General Motors does not compare with the Lower East

Side: the genius runs people away or attracts them as
their own genius finds corresponding influences: feeling
"out of place" is unnerving for anybody: practically:

this is a high floral season: pussyfoot clover has
shot up and died: common plaintain is mid-cone in
thready bloom: slight hawkweed is putting yellow

buttons a foot off the ground: woolly mullein is
breaking out halfway up into a flowering inferno:
for the gross showy, there is purple vetch stringing

up fields, chicory looking windy, butterflyweed too
early for butterflies, wild yellow daisies, and other
sanguine displays: it was today (7-8-75) a page ago:

today was Having Lunch with the Fucking Photography Committee
Day: pecan pie was a dollar a wedge· bavarian creme
pie, only 80¢: (that *only*'s going to have a different

tone when bcp is $1.60): the mt goes, how's it
going today: I go, it's going fine: the mt goes,
we going to get anything going today: I go, how's

it going with you: going fine, the mt goes: I go,
what do you say we get going: the mt goes, come:
one way to write is not for permanent improvement but

just to give the reader a place to be while he's there:
he might want to come back later and be there again:
even stuff written for long, arduous, out-of-time

contemplation and permanent improvement can hope for
nothing better than that: make an interesting place,
people will visit: there's just not that much call

these days for polished doldrums (that's doldrums with
a sea to shiny sea): people are interested in
trash: that's where pretension goes to take a spill:

could if anybody else would do anything he could: back
to the trash, back to this, this home away from home:
it's hard for a child to learn that adults are flawed,

even corrupt: this young country hasn't learned that
corruption is the way: when it learns that,
maybe it can accept it or change it: the people look

sad on the porches: the children play but seem puzzled:
the old ladies don't trust the street: the young men
and women, uncalled for, are unemployed: braggadocio:

you may be the type of person who can't understand
why anybody would want to write poetry, let alone
read it: that's where the reading mainly is, let

alone: most people would rather be a fountain than
a basin, for some reason: but as for writing, why,
it's like walking, you aren't working but you aren't

doing nothing: but walking this morning, I heard the
painter say to the kid, "You aren't allowed on the
ladder, period": allowed on the ladder: I took

yesterday off: why not work a day and rest a week:
I don't know if I had worked a week, but I rested a
day: I called it Knocking the Fucking Bitching

Off a Day Day: as a transcendental affirmationalist
I undergo throes complaining: I do better thinking
there must be some reason to go on living: bitching

can get you in the worst frame of mind: you think,
what can I find to bitch about today: and you can
find something: that's the leanest reassurance:

is a tree a concrete thing: right: I mean, maybe:
that is, it's a specific location and disposition:
not abstract: all right, all right: (who's talking):

it's also a microclimate: but in so many ways. it
absorbs radiation, it shades the ground, it moistens
the environment, it slows the wind: but then the

corner concrete (not abstract) is also a microclimate:
it bakes in the hot sun, an egg-frier: then there's
the black macadam and the white streak, minority white,

a climate in a climate: then there are the windy
corners (fairly abstract), puddles, marigolds: all
contribute microclimates to the high summation when

the fellow on the radio says, it's eighty-five degrees:
everything about works that way, from the dense local
to the synopsis: a waste is a terrible thing to mind:

we're getting a gospel singing group, The Rock of
Ages: what a very different effect would be The Ages
of Rock: this is 7-10: started back a way with

"you may be the type": I'm the typist: when the
going gets tough, the tough get going: I go warm up
the coffee: (it has worked its way up from the wind

through the waters, the leaves of bushes and branches,
tangles and brambles, risen to summits and made
space, rounded out the vision to the lay of land

and lands and now it looks into the human eye: what
is it: it is the viability, the coherence, that has
assumed disposition: nearly mute, having been mute a

while, it wants to have a program but fears the layout
of justice to each detail will deprive amelioration of
direction and force, that what is is so because it has

worked itself out through necessity: wisdom will not
fool with the just and fear assails the disruptive
song introduced to turn the balanced unbalanced right):

aggravated: can't handle the pile-up of phobias: can't
deal with tunnels, bridges, gaps: can't get around much
anymore: if you have a humidity problem, move to the

desert: burn the insides of your head out: want
to get away from pollution, but there's no nearest hospital:
try southern California, look out for the rattlesnakes:

Florida, hurricanes: Vermont, timothy in August and
the winter dreadful: well, well: it looks as if
paradise was built elsewhere: find a nice island, it's

waterless and fifty minutes by launch to the mainland:
had a lot of aggravation: contradictions going by in
arpeggios, obbligatos, cadenzas, droves: listen

to the swarm: but I don't care; I still know to
a hair what my desire is: contrarieties, swift and
heavy confluences, "whole" situations good and bad:

get a little crust: the defenseless are so generous
and kind: paint your mean streak: nothing banishes
fear like meanness: just a touch: a little whatfor:

aggressive is a nice adjective for up-and-coming young
men: but the noun is a little heartless: aggressive
means resistant to wilting and withering under trying

conditions: means willing to figure out ways to prevent
failure: means right in there: (get your poetical
omnibus of cozy statements and friendly feelings,

several dollars and nothing taxing): what animals
we are, Men Stinking: we can't fix our attention on
ourselves and stay sober: fellow in his big car

yesterday, drove up to the intersection and, bloop,
emptied his ashtray in the middle of the street: well,
if one cannot improve things, one must improve one's

view of things: but one must keep the improvement
slight, so one's views will not get too filthy with reality:
if one announced a deep or high improvement one would be

classified: though trash collector (lingo, junk talk,
street bitch) somewhat extraordinaire (I deal in pretty
high-level stuff) (I mean there are a lot of steets

I haven't been in) I don't make much of a good job
of it, nothing thorough or scientific, I just wallow
around like a caddis fly larva and let any loose

bit stick to me and my glue-like interest: I was
brought up on "I ain't got nary'un" instead of "I
don't have one.": but I (do) don't deal with lingo in

its fresh, dough-like origins but in its cast-offs,
worn-outs, stiff-and-thins, the used-up literary:
I like that because who would want to fool around

with anything live: just when words, all glare and
no energy, are cascading out of vital curvatures, I
go about and pick them up (seine them out) tinny

mementos: go to the ocean always at the same time, the
ocean will always be different: I used to think there
was something ahead of me, but now I think there is

nothing behind me: the noise level here is bel canto:
several children yelling, crying, agreeing and
disagreeing: a dull plane burring: the dog across

the street yapping furiously: cars burning through
the air, splitting, the tires thubbing the cracks in
the concrete: the record-player of the boy-house right

behind us at record level: cars rodding off from the
intersection or screeching off or screeching to a stop:
dishes rattling: water frying through the pipes: the

typewriter clacking: that's some of it at the moment:
it subsides, it rises, but it never goes away: Edison
was half-lucky when he got his ears pulled and couldn't

half hear thereafter: now, a man is yelling, hey, hey,
and a big-truck's motor has started: the dog is at
his high-excitement level, yipping: Royall Drive in

Winston-Salem was so quiet by comparison, maybe a car
an hour, the dogs loose, at least (unleashed) and nosing
quiet: Hanshaw, too, is better than this: anything is:

pile on that the stagnant, humid air, rated "unhealthy"
and the hanging cloudcover, two days old and scheduled
to hold: there are a number of other conditions

that promise no improvement: I wonder how people get
by and what they could want enough to give them the
strength to get by: whatever it is, I must be missing it:

this was supposed to be Judge the Fucking Photography
Contest Day but the rains, by the beautiful sea,
continued, and it was deemed better not to show one's

photos than to get them rainacid etched: so I made it Get
the Fucking Car Serviced Day and Try to Figure Out
Why the Fucking Accelerator Sticks: the importance

of a bright spot has not been grossly exaggerated:
there at the service station were the verbal
artifacts hanging on the wall, the appropriate

summation or penates of the place: "I know that you
believe you understand what you think I said but
I am not sure you realize that what you heard is not

what I meant:" or "We're too lazy to work and too
nervous to steal," (that's a literary steal) or, "As you
slide down the banister, etc. splinters the wrong, etc."

or, "Labor Charges — Per hour, $10.00; If you watch,
$12.50; If you help, $15.00; If you do the job,
$20.00": this has not been a good year for summers:

as long as I can lay my hand to it, I will try to
assuage the problem: live living it up down: shake
a tower (take a shower): as we were driving to the mainland

this afternoon, the accelerator kept sticking at fifty while
I was braking and shifting into neutral and roaring:
how scary! an unturnoffable car! unslowdownable!

but then when we got to Mary's, Bob fixed it for me:
greased the works, put the return spring in a tighter
notch: there was so much Saturday traffic, stacked up,

I couldn't imagine how I'd get back over the bridge:
we came home via the toll, Longport Bridge: how sweet
it was, to be in charge of idling, though the bridge opened:

the weather's so rainy and stormy you can't get your
astronauts up: birds can't fly dry: worms are out of
their holes: the cookies are bewithered with dew:

the towels are sticky, sour, and repulsive: every
dainty pussy's indoors: this is Aren't There a Lot of
Those Fucking Little Raindrops Today Day (7-13):

if I touch your balls, you will never forget me: if
I nip your clit, I will forever appear as an imagination
in your thoughts: if I only touch the fringe of the

hairy aura around your balls, so they shrink and,
crinkling, cringe, a ghostly spook will be on you,
haunting: or if I describe with the lightness of

a mind's lineation the expanded folding labia of
your whompus, you will bear forever the start of a
nearly actual surprise: if I mark you with a touchous

incision in your tenderest parts, and meanwhile hold
you with my probing eyes, you will never give my
presence up, a dwelling about you: you will wonder

& dream: you will search my lines for my line: in
your deepest moment with another, I will appear and,
possessing you, shoo you over the hills, the agony

and the glide: but since I don't need to ravish
more than a million, don't take it too seriously:
skirmishes: splinters: after a while, depression depresses:

one morning you see on a bright concrete
corner a stack of dog-do and you think, that must
be quite a pooch, but the sun bakes it and the next

morning the pooch seems smaller until one morning the
do is so tight, dry, and trivial the pooch is a poodle:
sum & tendency: (7-19): the prettiest day invited

thousands of shoobies to come to the beach, every
parking place car-solid, but early afternoon has
turned cloudy, windy, cooler, few raindrops, and the

shoobies are packing up their boxes, beach chairs,
umbrellas, etc. and heading back for the mainland:
"That's the way it goes" is the cheerful summary:

have fun: what, you mean toss the cares and worries
like a beachball, the way the cares and worries toss
us like a beachball! the very idea of having fun!

try to imagine it, just dropping the fears and severe
entertainments and letting the self sing with loss of
caution! sing into something like the delightful

terror of the salt-and-pepper shaker, scrambler or
tilt-a-whirl: what a security, to be able to taunt
terror: what a stability that hungers for disaster,

inferno, earthquake as no more than a sweet unsettling
while I, contrariwise, shaking dream on sweet ease:
oh for a security that thinks in years: oh for rock

underfoot: well, that is my pitiful, self-pitying
problem: I will spare you the details: or any
realization of languishing anguish: just remember

with air-conditioned cars the unnatural air can make
you think unnaturally: if you have a dog or baby in
the car, you must remember if you leave the car to roll

down the windows and let the warm air in: for the
closed windows that protected your coolness will hold
heat when the cooler stops: think unnaturally right:

disaster is natural: look at my face: some concession
to gravity: I knew this lady: she did everything for
her husband: she did everything for her children.

she said, sit down to the table: she had the most
beautiful voice, I mean as to tone and range and before
breakfast cooking stuff up: now, she bubbles belching

in terror and can't keep her tongue in: I can't stand
pretty beauty anymore: I can't stand any beauty that
doesn't sit and think her the most beautiful person

living: disaster is natural: I saw the legless
ward at the VA lots of times, diabetes gangrene
amputations, old boys: each carried a bottle of urine

under his wheelchair with a tube: like gas for the
motor: and just about everyone slouched over and
slept as deep as possible: there was the young

veteran, though: he burned up the halls and
shot the corners on one wheel: he had it down to
nothing how much breeze he could make of speed: oh,

the loft is high and rid of such: up in the sways,
nobody is holding on to keep from falling out of his
bed: farther along we'll understand why: it is not,

finally, perhaps, ingratitude: it is not, finally,
not celebration: it is that we do not understand,
now: it is that we cannot see beauty all the way

through: it is that we think we would be justified
in wanting it another way, permanent joy: a land
imagined where love would never be pulled away from

love: where mothers and fathers would know beatitude
and touch us with their unconditioned smiles: where
tenderness would be so high it would transmit

light: and love of lovers would be a continual
music, reconciliations like breeze music: the rivers would
be flowing light and trees would sway with the fruit of

light: we do not understand why a place like this
would yield out no design: then, should our beauty
be the dream of the place and have nothing to do with

actual fellows: or should our beauty find itself
somehow perfect in the harelip, the crazy fascination
of cross-eyes or in the wild song of the cancer-mad:

our beauty, our beauty: on what shoal or shelf, ledge
or cloud will it lie down, dwelling beyond rust and moth,
so beyond it will know the worm and have no cognizance

thereof: the famous don't care for change, except
the change that nudges them to greater fame: you can beat
up on the ocean but not beat it up: you can beat it

up a little, you can splash or scrinch it: low tide
exposes the flank of the jetty, four strata to view:
lowest, black mussels: next, barnacles: next, seaweed:

then, sun country, naked: though the strata are
discernible, they are not insistent: here and there
barnacles lock under a boulder higher than seaweed:

and here and there seaweed clumps right down into the
barnacle bed: orders that permit variety (and adjustment)
are sort of casual, optimum dispositions: exactly the

way my poem is or means to be: sometimes a life has so
much thrust and verve, it has to be killed back and
back, until killing back becomes a way of doing things,

and then the verve becomes so great only killing ends
it: so, depression is often the sign of too much life,
but not coming through: the withering is the "show"

that holds life in: when it is a life one thinks should
not come through, then it is terribly troublesome, and
one must find ways, bowling or pooling, that will let

enough through to keep the rest in: then, depression can
be increased by the knowledge of life lost: it is not
a tangle susceptible to easy untangling, but the most

reliable, partial untangling is to do something physical:
do not languish, weakening with the loss and holding in:
getting something out, even if not in the form it desired

release in, will often permit the grip to ease and the
flow, a slow flow, to move: Abby knows a lot but I
doubt she knows much about this: consult your physician:

I say do something physical even when I know that is
absolutely the hardest thing to do: but force yourself:
make a daily schedule, or weekly, that includes several

things, walks, showers, hangings-loose, hair combings,
nail cleanings, and then into all the other things:
showers are excellent because depressed people let

themselves get dirty and that depresses them: even if
you get a sniffle or two, even a cold, at first, begin
a regime of showers: touch yourself here and there

afterwards with a dab of powder or cologne: strike a
figure or two before the mirror: the tension will
sometimes erase wrinkles or re-arrange them: I met

a man this year who has suffered from the sharp
pains of gas for ten years, and he didn't know what I
told him, that you can take a single swallow of water

and dislodge the bubble enough to stop the pain: that
was good news to him, something I discovered: but, of
course, the water doesn't get rid of the bubble: I've

found that walking about a bit will sometimes loosen
the bind enough to free the bubble: also, slowly
twisting the body from side to side will sometimes bring

relief: if you've never experienced that uncomfortable
tightness with the splinters of pain, you won't realize
how important this message is: tuck it away in the

wrinkles, grooves, or furrows of your ready remedies:
the message, not the tightness: I'm really interested
in you: I mean I think I'm more interested in you than

you are in me: maybe I'm interested in you because I
want you to be interested in me: or maybe I'm just
interested in having you think of me as someone

interested in you: though I've never met you, I'll say
this, my interest in you is no vaguer than my knowledge
of you: featherless biped, naked ape: one of us: all

the gulls with nothing chasing the gull with something:
a likely story: a review came today (which is, by the
way, 7-21) that said I fall far short of Stevens: I

guess that means you couldn't hang your hat on mine: I
never tried to fall far long of him: I have great
respect for Mr. Stevens, but he is not as sobering as

the ocean: after watching two hours of Flintstones, it's
unwackying to get right down to the surf and see it
rolling and busting in: there are so many actions and

yet they are so simple and similar: the actions do not
resist the intelligence (poems do), in fact, declare
themselves openly in big summary waves: it's not hard

to tell what is happening, though it is of course quite
past calculation: other men are my man: I don't like
fancy colors or big cigars; I like loudmouths that

pretend to care for the people: I don't care for the
people much: I don't know many of them: but I mean to
care for the people: I really am fond of all the

minorities, except the rich: I have sympathy even for
them: they are deprived of the right to earn a living:
they know people see them as rich, not as people proper.

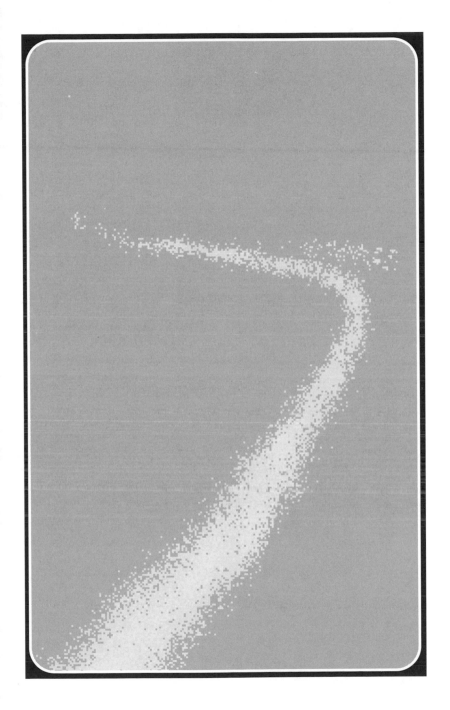